Smart Money with Purpose

Joe R. Kesler

LIBERATING THE GOODNESS
OF MONEY IN YOUR LIFE

This book is for educational purposes only and should not be relied upon to make important financial or other decisions. Please consult a professional for investing, legal, accounting or tax guidance. Any opinions expressed are those of the author and do not represent the views of any other organization.

All references from THE HOLY BIBLE, NEW INTERNATIONAL VERSION ®, NIV ® Copyright © 1973,1978,1984,2011 by Biblica, Inc. ™
Used by permission. All rights reserved worldwide.

© 2014 by Joe R. Kesler. All Rights Reserved. No part of this book may be reproduced in any form without permission in writing from the author.

ISBN: 1499162510
ISBN 13: 9781499162516

Library of Congress Control Number: 2014907254
CreateSpace Independent Publishing Platform
North Charleston, South Carolina

All websites listed herein are accurate at the time of publication, but may change in the future or cease to exist. The listings of website references are resources and do not imply author endorsement of the site's entire contents. Groups and organizations are listed for informational purposes and listing does not imply endorsement of their activities.

To my wife Nancy, my best friend and adventurer who liberated me to enjoy the goodness of life. Thanks for your belief in this project and your never ending support.

To my children Bryan, David, Benjamin, Bethany and Sarah: Behold your inheritance.

And, to the many friends who have attended small group sessions with me covering the material in this book over the years, I want to say thank you. Your supportive comments and feedback on its impact on your lives have given me the energy to complete this project. I especially want to thank Chris Caldwell for his patient, but regular encouragement to get it done. And to Chad and Fenesa, Penny, Marty and Robin, Andrew and Jacqueline, Chris, Tom and Dixie, Nick, Alex and Jesse, I want to shout out a special thank you for being the final group to review the material before press time. Also, I must thank my good friend Randy, whose able Bible teaching, conversations and friendship over the years gave me many of the ideas for the material in this book. Thanks also to Rachel for being a patient editor in helping to make this a more readable book.

Finally, I want to thank the many outstanding people who allowed me to fulfill a calling in the honorable profession of community banking. Thanks to the directors of the banks I have served in for their support for my leadership that gave me the experience necessary to write this book, the loyal customers I've been privileged to serve and learn from, and the many co-workers that have become my close friends and counselors. It's been a wonderful life!

Thank you all.

Contents

Introduction vii
How to Use this Book xvii
My Journey xix
Part I The Spiritual Side of Money 1
   1. Attitude Readjustment: Embracing the
      Goodness of Wealth 3
   2. The Deceitfulness of Money 21
   3. The Foundation: Putting the Power of
      Purpose in Your Financial Plan 39
Part II Your Relationship with Money 57
   4. Transforming Your Relationship with Money from the
      Inside Out 59
   5. Raising Your Money Consciousness to Live the
      Abundant Life 85
   6. Children and Houses and Cars, Oh My! Managing Money
      Successfully in Marriage 103
Part III Building Wealth 121
   7. Debt: The Good, the Bad and the Ugly 123
   8. 9 Habits of Successful Investing 141
   9. Joyful Generosity 161
Part IV Your Legacy 177
   10. Inheritance: Passing It On 179
Conclusion Where Do We Go From Here? 193
Appendix A Smart Money with Purpose Report Card 197
Notes 203

Introduction

Moreover, when God gives any man wealth and possessions, and enables him to enjoy them, to accept his lot and be happy in his work—this is a gift from God.
                                                    Ecclesiastes 5:1

"I *really* want to read your book when it's finished!" I've been surprised to hear the passion in that comment many times over the past couple of years from people in every walk of life. I've never written a book before, and personal finance is a crowded space. So it has taken me aback somewhat to find so many people who have a hunger for a book that sets out to connect their relationship with money with their desire to live an intentional and purposeful life. While not everyone cares about every aspect of finance, I've found almost universal interest in questions about our relationship with money. Some wrestle with the compatibility of money and spirituality:
- Can I enjoy money without losing my soul?
- Are spirituality and affluence compatible?
- Is it okay to want more money?

Other questions are more practical and personal:
- How can my spouse and I get on the same page with our finances?

- I don't like my job. What do I need to do financially before I set out to start my own business?
- Will I ever get out of debt?
- How can I accumulate enough money to pursue my real passion without having to work for a paycheck?

In my 36 years of working with customers in community banks, I have met with wealthy entrepreneurs with net worth in the millions as well as families under a crushing debt burden. With rare exception, it makes little difference what the circumstances are: everyone struggles with some aspect of money. I have also had the privilege of providing financial counseling in several churches and have found money problems creating anxiety in both rich and poor Christians alike. My conclusion from both my banking world and my church world is that our relationship with money is not only troubled, but first and foremost, a spiritual issue.

Living in harmony with money is elusive in our culture because the ways we have traditionally been taught to deal with money problems simply don't satisfy in the long run. Churches tend to focus on bringing in a speaker who will teach a formulistic self help process of six or seven steps to gain financial nirvana. The teacher may have had a terrible life experience with debt, so he spends the bulk of the time teaching about the evils of debt. Your marriage is a mess? Then get out of debt. Problems at work? Get out of debt. Whatever the situation, much of today's counsel in churches is to get out of debt and follow somebody's simplistic plan regardless of the wisdom of the process for their unique circumstances. That's a missed opportunity because a financial crisis is really an opportunity to help someone build a core spiritual foundation that is in accord with God's calling and purpose for their life.

Money counselors outside the church are usually not much different. They encourage setting goals, saving more, spending less, buying life insurance and, of course, paying off debt. But these actions alone aren't enough to gain contentment and a joyful life. These external changes will only bring peace if there is also an internal transformation that aligns your view of money with your internal wiring and purpose. In short, you don't have to serve money and be subject to confusion about its proper place in your life. Instead, it is possible for money to be *your* servant, a tool to be used to further your highest purposes and calling in life. However, developing a new mindset that aligns money with your life goals may require an internal makeover including an understanding of how we are wired to handle money. External changes may also be required to find peace, but only after they are brought into focus by a new understanding of money's purpose in our lives.

A Diagnostic Tool for the Soul

Money is first of all a valuable diagnostic tool about the state of our spiritual health. In fact, money is a window into our soul unlike any other. It provides a bridge where our internal self--our spirit--engages the external world. For instance, in a Christian context, we might fool even ourselves with most elements of worship. We can sing hymns without really worshiping, act very interested in a sermon when our mind is wandering or take communion without really engaging. But when the offering plate is passed, it's one place in a worship service where most of us come face to face with the question of whether we believe all this or not. Emotions that convince us we love Jesus one minute can suddenly grow cold in the face of parting with some of our hard-earned money with real bills at home to be paid.

In fact, the spiritual insight into our relationship with money is far from limited to our charitable giving. As a community banker I have been fascinated with how the lessons on money learned in the Scriptures are validated everyday in the real world of commerce. Vain attempts to find meaning in things and experiences lead us all to make poor financial decisions. For example, one common mistake I have seen many people make is buying into the belief that a big house will bring real significance to their lives. They over-leverage their balance sheet with debt and end up, in essence, with a big house, and an empty, stress-filled life. In fact, I have seen it all on Main Street: overspending, hoarding, investing in get rich quick schemes, guilt over having money and even obsession with money. But, at the same time, I've discovered some who have harnessed their relationship with money and are able to use it to accomplish their larger purpose in life. I'm convinced that a close look at our relationship with money will reveal a lot about the state of our soul and open us up to see the need to transform some aspects of our thinking.

Integrated Advice

This book represents a long term goal of mine to pull together my two worlds. As both a community bank CEO and a long term lay leader in churches, I want to offer integrated advice that is effective in the real world of finance and consistent with the teachings of the Bible and inner transformation. As a banker, I may have been able to help many people address common external problems such as refinancing 28% credit card debt into a 6% home equity loan. That offers immediate relief to my customers, but usually time and circumstances do not allow me to go deeper into the real heart issues of why they ended up deep in high interest debt. If not properly addressed, these same customers might be back to the bank in another year with not only the new real estate loan unpaid, but having also run up the credit card debt again due to a lack of self control. I've never relished compartmentalizing financial advice by separating personal finance from heart issues. But it is usually only in the context of the church that I am completely free to go much deeper with financial counsel and help members understand the connection between their inner spiritual state and their finances. This book will bring those two worlds together to offer sound financial advice, but with a spiritual foundation that can put you on the path to a holistic approach to managing your finances.

Why should you Read this Book?

There is no shortage of books and study guides about money management in the marketplace and a new entry needs to have a compelling reason for asking you for your time. I can assure you that there is a lot of good and bad material published on money management. I've read many of the Christian books as well as many volumes of secular books on personal finance. You would be wise to read other authors on this important topic if you have the time, but one value of this book is that it will give you some of the best money practices for gaining peace with your finances--all in one place.

I have confidence in making this claim because I have had a lot of passionate encouragement to write a book from those who have gone through this material in small groups with me. I've seen marriages strengthened, financial novices gain wisdom and worldviews about money changed in a positive, joyful direction as a result of this material. It is valuable to spend time rethinking a dominant influence in our lives such as money. This book will explore the topic all the way from a theological to a practical level.

Many who have applied this material found it leads to a richer, more intentional life.

Secondly, I think you will appreciate that the book's principles have been forged, not in academic ivory towers or in the high rises of Wall Street, but where real people live. I have to function in the world where people live and work, on Main Street. As a CEO, I've had to face the daily challenges of running a business that requires a lot of tough decisions. I've tried to balance that toughness with being big hearted in dealing with the customers, community members and employees I interact with on a daily basis. Leading a business or giving financial counsel requires a lot of discernment. Those daily experiences have helped me gain wisdom in walking a fine line between showing compassion while not becoming an enabler when it comes to money matters. I've tried to write with that same balance of being driven by a heart that wants you to have peace with your finances, but that is tough minded and challenging to an unhealthy relationship with money.

Did I mention that you might also become wealthier if you read this book? Part of my banking career has included being responsible for the insurance and wealth management divisions in the banks I have managed. That responsibility has also given me a lot of insiders' knowledge into some of the conflicts of interest that financial advisors must deal with that impact you as consumers of financial products and services. While most financial advisors are ethical, any investor still needs to be aware of the compensation practices in these industries that might tempt the advisor to put you into products that maximize their commission, but are not necessarily in your best interest. I'll reveal some of these inside secrets that you should be aware of as you accumulate money and turn to others for advice. Good stewardship of what you accumulate includes being wise about some of these potential hindrances to achieving your financial goals.

The book's approach to financial management could be visualized as a giant redwood tree that has a complex web of invisible roots supporting the strength and beauty we see above the ground. While we can't see the roots, without them there is no way the tree would be able to withstand storms, grow and provide us with such beauty and shade. Similarly, the external fruits of a well ordered financial life--generosity, investments, low stress--do not happen without a lot of invisible beliefs and practices supporting the prosperity. Unlike most other books on money, we'll look not only at the visible manifestation of living at peace with your finances, but also at the root causes of it.

I write from a Christian perspective that the Bible provides important revelation on the topic of money in our lives. If you do not believe in the Christian message then you might wonder if the book has anything of value for you. The church I attend usually begins each service with a comment something along these lines, "This is a safe place where you don't have to share our convictions to be our friend and process the unique claims of Christianity." Similarly, I would encourage you to join me in considering the wisdom found in the Bible even if you don't hold to my religious tradition. My experience with people who aren't religious has been that they are not opposed to religion, but they just don't see the point of it. But then a crisis happens where they find their own worldview unable to answer fundamental questions about life. They become open to a reexamination of what Christianity says that might help make sense of their world. Financial stress can be one of those events that open us up to new ways of looking at life so we can experience renewal and growth. If that's you, my prayer is that this book might offer some surprising answers to your financial situation. That said, I am the first to admit that I have learned from secular writers in my journey, and I will reference several in the book. Common grace, a Christian doctrine that all people are gifted with insight because of our common creation in the image of God, is obviously true in the area of finances. However, I make some unique claims regarding money that are based on Biblical truths. I encourage you to consider them and test them to see if they help you make better sense of your world of money.

How the Book is Organized

The book is divided into four sections. In Part I we will look closely at the spiritual side of money. This section is based on the belief that our lives ought to be lived in harmony with our deepest religious beliefs and life purposes. We'll venture into some theological waters where we lay the ground work for an ethic regarding money that will be the basis for financial joy whatever level of affluence we ultimately achieve. In Part II we explore our relationship with money, examine how it becomes broken, and steps we can take to get it back on the right track. Part III then builds on the prior two sections to show the best ways to manage the fruit of a well ordered financial life that is spending less than is being earned. We look at the three uses for excess cash flow of debt repayment, investing and charitable giving. Finally, Part IV looks at our legacy. We'll discuss how to think about inheritance and how to prepare to leave it all behind for the greatest good and glory to God.

Final Notes

I include a lot of stories. For obvious reasons, I've changed the names and details of the characters to protect their privacy. Also, this book contains a lot of financial wisdom, but it is not intended to be an investment, legal, accounting or tax guide. Your specific situation will be unique and you should consult competent professionals for guidance on your financial plan.

For those of you who will be using this book in a small group context, I've included a short discussion in the next section on how to use the book if you're the group leader. I've also included a short version of my journey in the world of personal finances in the section after the one on how to use the book. If you'd like to know a bit more about who I am you can read it, or if you want to get started you can just skip ahead to chapter one.

If you have questions as you read this material, or if you want to go deeper into a particular topic, I encourage you to visit my website at http://smartmoneywithpurpose.com. I'd love to hear from you and I list additional resources there on the topics discussed in the book.

Coffee with George Bailey

As you begin this journey, just think of this book as a chance to sit down for a cup of coffee to discuss your finances with the Jimmy Stewart banker character, George Bailey, in the movie, "It's a Wonderful Life." It's a safe place to reveal your financial struggles and get some advice from your friendly community banker who wants you to have peace with your finances. We'll have a great discussion about you and your finances.

How to Use this Book

I am a big believer in the value of small groups when trying to recalibrate our financial lives. Some very successful lending models use a principle which is called "solidarity lending" in which group members encourage one another. The Grameen Bank, for example, has been a very successful lending model in helping raise people out of poverty through micro loans and solidarity groups. Similarly, groups like "Underearners Anonymous" use group dynamics successfully to deal with money issues. This book can be read by you alone, but it was written with the hope that it will normally be used in the context of a small group of people who are authentic enough to openly discuss their struggles with money. I know the value is significant when a group comes together in a safe place to mutually encourage each other in changing the way they deal with their finances. This will involve a willingness to be open about your relationship with money and a commitment to read the chapters and answer the questions at the end of each chapter.

What I have found helpful in leading small group studies on these topics is to lay out some ground rules as follows:

- What is said in the group stays in the group. Confidentiality is critical when it comes to discussions about money and personal struggles. Everyone should acknowledge their agreement to this rule.
- I do not recommend full disclosure of personal finances in the group setting. The reason for this relates to the

powerful influence money can have on us. If, for example, a doctor begins sharing about how difficult it is to live on a six figure salary, it suddenly becomes hard for the individual making $25,000 to relate and easy for a judgmental attitude to develop. What I recommend is that you try to restrict your comments to percentages. For example, "I am spending 25% of my income on housing," or "my loan on my house is about 95% of its value," are ways to share about your personal finances that everyone can relate to without separating yourself from others in a totally different economic class.

- The small group needs to be a safe place to share. If someone in the group sells financial products, that needs to be disclosed and that individual needs to assure the group leader that he or she will not use the group as a place to peddle their products. This can be stressed to the group so everyone knows that it is not a forum for sales leads for anyone.
- A willingness to approach the book with an openness to change actual behavior will manifest itself in doing the assignments laid out. There will be many things in this book that are intellectually interesting, but if there is no focus and commitment to change then nothing more than gaining a new way of looking at money will be gained. So I would encourage you as you read this book to be open to having others hold you accountable for taking action when appropriate.
- At the end of each chapter I have provided several focus questions. If you are reading this in a group you should allocate time for discussing the questions and doing the exercises.

My Journey

My own interest in the spiritual perspective of money started in the late '70s when somebody gave me an Inter Varsity Press book called *Rich Christians in an Age of Hunger*.[i] I had never really thought seriously about the connection between God and money until I read that book and it challenged me to think hard about what the Bible says about the poor. It included an argument for the government's role in redistributing wealth from the rich that sounded reasonable. Sometime later, someone gave me a book written in response called *Productive Christians in an Age of Guilt Manipulators*.[ii] It was the polar opposite perspective! My intellectual juices were swimming. It was a confusing time for me because both authors came from a Christian perspective, but arrived at very different conclusions. After these two books I was hooked on the topic and realized that God had a lot to say about money and I had much to learn. Partly because of these books I pursued a calling in the banking industry.

Then in the 80's I had a crisis early in my career when I attended a Christian conference in Chicago. During one of the intermissions I wandered through the exhibit hall and found myself at a table with literature on banking. As I talked to the vendors, I quickly realized that they were promoting the position that all lending at interest was condemned by God and that the entire banking industry was morally wrong. Being a committed Christian, I had to take that challenge seriously and look for a new line of work if they were correct. The shock of that conversation led me on a research mission to eventually rediscover the revolutionary teachings that came out of the Reformation. I discovered that lending at interest was widely condemned by the church until, through the influence of John Calvin and others, the correct understanding of immoral lending was explained as lending *to the poor* at interest. Lending to others, rather than being a crime, was actually considered a part of God's blessing in the Scriptures (Deut. 28:12). I noted that even the year of Jubilee, with the provision for forgiveness of debt, showed that lending was an established part of the Israelite culture. Lending for productive purposes was not only allowed, it created a tremendous surge of wealth and poverty alleviation as previously unproductive resources were now allowed to be employed in legitimate business arrangements. However, lending to the poor at interest was clearly wrong and to be avoided. My banking career was not only salvaged, I was now convinced it was a sacred calling, even an act of loving my neighbor because of the good that occurs when resources are productively allocated.

As I continued to study, I learned about the historical roots of the Protestant work ethic. I was fascinated by the explosion of wealth that occurred during and after the Reformation because of these "religious" beliefs. The idea that religion and commerce never met was destroyed. I was fascinated that all of life was to be seen as sacred and not just activities in the church. I began to see that much of contemporary Christian financial literature had missed this truth.

After gaining this intellectual and spiritual foundation for a banking career I realized I had been wired uniquely for this calling when I tried to pass the CPA exam for the first time in 1984. Never having been much of a student, I was shocked when I ended up with special honors for scoring in the top 100 out of around

70,000 that took that particular exam. As it dawned on me that I had scored in the top one tenth of one percent of a fairly smart group, I realized maybe God had uniquely formed me for a ministry helping others with money problems. I began to apply myself with more rigor and picked up two graduate degrees in business to fill in some knowledge gaps. This prepared me for a variety of career opportunities including the chance to run two good sized community banks as CEO. Having reviewed literally thousands of financial statements over the years, I have discerned patterns of financial behavior of what works in life and what doesn't. At the same time I found a real hunger in churches for integrating personal finance with the core teachings of Jesus and the Christian faith. It was natural to try to meet this need by teaching classes and small groups on the principles of finance that I had found in the Scriptures that I also saw validated in my banking job. Having done this type of teaching for years, I decided it was time to set some of these thoughts in writing, not only for the supportive church groups that have encouraged me to do so, but also for my five children for whom I want to provide a record of the truths of money management their dad has learned over the years.

My hope is that some of what I have learned over the years in my journey studying and dealing with money issues will be helpful to you in your unique situation. I look forward to sharing some of the things I have learned, but would love to get feedback from you too. I would really enjoy hearing from you on my blog at:

http://smartmoneywithpurpose.com.

PART I

The Spiritual Side of Money

CHAPTER 1

Attitude Readjustment: Embracing the Goodness of Wealth

"Make all you can, save all you can, give all you can,"
John Wesley, 18th century founder of the Methodist church

"And the gold of that land is good."
Genesis 2:12

The man sitting across from me was telling everyone at the dinner table, "I know it is possible to live abundantly without money." I was having a hard time processing his comments, but the way he told the story and his body language told me that his story was true. Fourteen years ago he said he pulled out of his pocket all of his earthly wealth -thirty dollars- and left it in a phone booth. He had not used any currency for any purpose ever since that decisive moment. Did you know that such a thing was possible? Someone living in American society who not only doesn't use money, but doesn't even believe in it? Thinks it's an illusion. I did not until I had the chance to hear his story.

It was an engaging conversation as he was not an uneducated freeloader coasting off of the hard work of others. He was actually a very articulate, well educated, middle-aged man who grew up in a conservative church, but grew disenchanted partly because he didn't see anyone taking Jesus' teachings on money seriously. His lifelong spiritual quest had led him to conclude that we are meant to live simply and without money, like the animals do. He illustrated his belief by pointing out that if bears are hungry they eat berries that they find, but don't pay for them. Money does not exist in nature and yet the natural world thrives. He is consistent with his beliefs by living in the moment. He looks for food when he is hungry, lives in a cave when he is not traveling, and he is not afraid to miss a meal once in awhile.

Several things stood out about the conversation. First, I've known a lot of people who are uncomfortable around money, but I had never met anyone who had made a decision to live their life consistent with a belief that money is, if not necessarily evil, at best an illusion. The strength of character to actually live a life without the influence of money made me appreciate his iron will. But, I also found others' reaction to him most interesting. Some were in awe, almost putting him on a pedestal as a hero to be imitated because he is saying no to something they sense is evil in its essence. However, he also creates guilt among these same admirers because they know they are unable to break themselves free of money's gravitational pull and its influence on all they do. Others I have talked to about this man's lifestyle are angered by his life and feel he is living off the productive resources of others and should be shunned rather than praised. Personally, I found his story a great opportunity to engage in conversations about money because his unusual life does move people emotionally one way or another. It can expose the stress fractures in many folk's philosophy of money when opposing sides discuss his life. This experience confirmed why it's important to begin our discussion about money, not with financial tactics, but by first laying a clear Christian foundation.

The Necessity of a Christian Worldview about Money and Affluence

It's no mystery why many American Christians might be uncomfortable with money. The Scriptures are clear that we are to be concerned for the welfare of the poor. Economic facts make those of us with money who wrestle with living a Christ-honoring life squirm. What exactly is our duty? Most Americans live on about $90.00 a day[iii] while 2.45 billion people live on less than $2.00 a day.[iv] Over 1.3 billion people live on less than $1.25 daily.[v] These types of statistics along with the Bible's emphasis on caring for the poor leave Christians feeling embarrassed and guilty over their wealth, completely unable to enjoy the prosperity they have been given. Given the joy that is found in our reconciliation to God, this pervasive guilt cannot be the life God calls us to. And yet, we must find peace by living with a clean conscience, reconciling what we read in the Bible about poverty with the material blessings we enjoy.

Let me illustrate this point. A number of years ago I attended a debate on economics between two pastors. I will never forget the way it ended. After a healthy discussion debating whether the Bible taught a socialistic economic system or an economy with more individual freedom, there was an opportunity for questions. The pastor promoting the socialistic duty of Christians to live a life of poverty was asked why he drove a "snappy little Toyota" when there are so many starving people in the world. He turned red faced and admitted that he did drive the car, but very defensively pointed out that he only owned two pair of shoes! He then went on the attack and asked the questioner, somewhat piously, how many pair of shoes he had? The questioner didn't miss a beat and responded that it was the pastor's theology that didn't allow him to enjoy anything representing affluence, not his! Then the questioner asked him why he didn't ride a bicycle instead to be more consistent with his theology! It was a bit uncomfortable, but nevertheless, the point was made. No matter how simply we attempt to live, we can always find others much poorer than ourselves. If we believe that possessions and wealth in excess of what the poorest own show our lack of concern for the poor, we have consigned ourselves to a joyless life of misery and guilt.

The formal philosophical term that could describe this pastor's ethics is utilitarianism. This philosophy holds that the proper course of action is always the one that maximizes happiness and reduces suffering for the most people. It sounds good on the surface. But, one big problem with this philosophy lies in that no one will ever be allowed to delight in the good things God has given in this world to enjoy. The pastor in the debate took self-righteous pride in the fact that he only had two pairs of shoes while others had many more, but agonized in guilt over driving a car because of the bondage of his philosophy. What a pitiful way to live. Furthermore, it's not biblical. The Bible is full of examples of God wanting his people to live lives of joy in an affluent land "flowing with milk and honey," (Ex 33:3) even when the poor were still with them. Jesus himself was criticized by the Pharisees of his day for being a glutton and a drunkard because he came "eating and drinking" in the midst of suffering. (Luke 7:34) The event that seemed to turn Judas to betray Jesus was the breaking of expensive perfume to pour on Jesus that could have been "sold and given to the poor." (Matt 26:7) Utilitarianism that agonizes over spending or saving any money because there are people suffering in other parts of the world is not only unbiblical; it is counterproductive. Investments that create wealth have lifted one billion people out of poverty since 1990.[vi] This can only be done if capital is accumulated and not all given away. In fact, the goal of eliminating poverty in the 21st century is something that is seriously discussed today. Giving help directly to the poor has a place as a Christian discipline that we will discuss in chapter 9, but it is not the primary means of poverty alleviation for those serious about this important topic. Nor does living like a hermit contribute in any way to the elimination of poverty.

The point is *not* that greed does not exist. It does, and we will discuss it in depth in the next chapter when we explore the deceitfulness of wealth. However, I start with a proper joy in abundance because guilt over wealth and its enjoyment can be as sad and destructive as greed among Christians.

God's View of Money

Let us not be so embarrassed of money being useful that we forget God created the world. He did not suddenly become distracted by something, turn back around and notice that man had invented something called money! In fact, from the earliest chapters of the Bible it's clear that God had a plan for the use of money. In addition to the creation, He also pronounced money "good." It's right there in Genesis 2:12, the 43rd verse in the Bible, where God pronounces for only the eighth time that something is good--gold. Gold has always been a metaphor for money even in our current day. So the starting point for any discussion about the Bible's view of money must begin with the premise that God sees it, along with the rest of His creation, as something good.

So money is good. But here is the million dollar question (pardon the pun): Is it acceptable for the Christian or anyone else to "want more money?" And here is the clear and unambiguous answer; yes it can be morally right to want more money! But, I would like to clarify that just like any other virtue, this one can turn into something ugly called greed and idolatry. As I've said, we'll get to that in later chapters, but for now let's just talk about the virtuous side of wanting and making more money. This is a critical point for you to have settled in your mind if you want to gain peace before God as you become more prosperous. Stay with me on this. You will either miss your potential in making money or you will feel guilty at your success if you fail to resolve this issue within your soul.

You can be very happy with your life, even content with a grateful heart for all the wonderful blessings around you, and yet simultaneously want more. In fact, if your business meets my needs, I want you to want more because it means that you will be willing to work hard for me to meet my needs. To bring this into focus, let's look at the individual who doesn't want more money. For example, the retired worker who sits on the beach all day feeling quite content is unlikely to do anything for you or me. On the other hand, if you are struggling to meet all your obligations each month and have a desire to make more money you are more than likely to figure out a way to meet some need I have so I will pay you more. I like that. You're willing to meet my needs and I'm happy to say thank you by giving you money. Think what a poverty-stricken world this would be if no one wanted to make more money by meeting other's needs.

Try this exercise to help understand in a practical way how good it is that our neighbors are motivated by money. Think about your morning routine and how many people are working for you just to get you from bed to your workplace. You get up and brush your teeth. Could you build a toothbrush on your own? What about the toothpaste? I don't even know what's in it, let alone how they get that paste into that little tube. I usually shave with an electric razor. I would have no idea how to put one of them together, but I sure am happy that I've got thousands of people working everyday to think about how to make my shave smoother and closer just so I'll buy a new razor every few years from them. Or, think about breakfast for a minute. I've gotten used to having blueberries or blackberries on my cereal. How many workers are there who make sure I can have fruit on my cereal even in the middle of winter? I sure am glad they are motivated to give me fresh fruit in winter months. For most of human history fresh fruit in winter was a luxury that even the richest kings couldn't have enjoyed, but I take it for granted. And then there's the daily commute. How many steel workers, tire workers, miners and autoworkers were there involved in making my ride smooth? If I had to make a car on my own, I'd be walking. But even walking I rely on people who are motivated by making and selling shoes. I think you get the point. It's not surprising that Adam Smith, who first explained this invisible hand, meeting our daily needs, began as a religious philosopher before he became an economist.[vii] The connection between economics and the moral virtue of loving our neighbor is unmistakable to the observant.

It's important to remember that wealth is good because it comes from God. Deut 8:18 says, "But remember the Lord your God, for it is He who gives you the ability to produce wealth, and so confirms his covenant…" As God blesses our efforts to meet our neighbor's needs by giving us wealth, we are to remember Him and his covenant of love for us in all our commerce. But as we determine ways to meet our neighbor's needs, we are faced with the ethics of making a profit.

Getting Comfortable with the Profit Motive

I live in a beautiful little town tucked in mountains. You might have seen the movie that put Missoula on the map called, *A River Runs Through It*. Not only is Missoula physically beautiful, but it is also a town full of socially conscious individuals who seek to make the world a better place. Some have estimated that Missoula has the largest per capita number of non-profit organizations in the United States. Now nobody should have a problem with non-profit organizations *per se*. In fact, I have served on the boards of various non-profits my entire career. However, my sense is that there is sometimes an arrogance that flows out of the non-profit sector concerning anything that is rooted in making a profit. In this world view, the services being offered by businesses are tainted, possibly unjust and generally untrustworthy because of the profit motive.

This worldview assumes a dichotomy of spheres. There's the business world where profits rule and morality is a distant second if it exists at all. It is a place where profits disrupt ethical decisions resulting in ugly greed and selfishness. The profit motive is assumed to undermine all relationships that aren't transactional. It is the kind of world that Jesus would speak against if he were present. On the other hand, the non-profit sphere is romanticized as one of public service, family, community. It is assumed that because of the lack of a corrupting profit motive, the non-profit world is the only place where moral principles thrive.

The problem with this dualistic view is that it is naïve and incorrect in its assumptions of both worlds. I worked in government in the first few years of my career and while there are clearly many immoral, greedy scoundrels in the world of business, I can attest that they also exist in the parts of society not driven by the need to create a profit. For the follower of Christ, there does not need to be any difference in behavior in either the business world or the non-profit world. As the CEO of a profitable bank I can be just as concerned for my staff, customers, community and shareholders as I am for the stakeholders I am accountable to as a director of a non-profit corporation I might sit on. I'm the same person and I carry the same values wherever I go. Or, for the ethically challenged, selfishness and rivalry can exist just as easily in churches as on Wall Street. The human heart without grace will create havoc in any environment. The heart transformed by grace can, on the other hand, bring healing to either type of institution.

Moreover, if the profit motive is a corrupting factor, then we must condemn the poor widow that seeks to save money by taking advantage of the Groupon deal at the local grocery. There is in essence no difference between trying to hold down the grocery bill and the president of Boeing trying to locate a new production plant in a lower cost state or country. A union president trying to achieve the best agreement for his members is no different than the businessman trying to lower his cost of production. In fact, every rational person operates out of self interest. In my own industry, for example, it is reported that nonprofit credit union CEOs make more money than for profit community bank CEOs.[viii] That would be odd if you accepted the premise that non-profit institutions are staffed with individuals above self interest. Similarly, the American Institute of Philanthropy has scanned IRS information to come up with the 25 highest paid charitable CEO's. They ranged all the way from $774,000 to $2,207,000 in 2013.[ix]

The logical question is when does legitimate self interest become selfishness? From a Christian worldview, self interest should not be condemned *per se*, it is a trait of man created in the image of God and acting as a good steward. *Self interest* is when someone is trying to protect their own interests, but they also have their eye on helping their neighbor. No less a giant of the Christian faith than C.S. Lewis frequently wrestled with this question of the proper place of self interest versus the sin of selfishness. Some maintain that Mark 8:35-36 is Lewis's most frequently quoted passage,[x] "For whoever wants to save their life will lose it, but whoever loses their life for me and for the gospel will save it. What good is it for someone to gain the whole world and forfeit their soul." Lewis never dismissed the idea of heavenly rewards, but he knew the paradox of practicing selflessness (losing one's life), but getting rewards (saving one's life) might be a problem to sort out intellectually. The pressure is relieved by carefully distinguishing between selfishness and self interest. *Selfishness* is a corruption of the fall and is where one makes decisions based on what's best for me regardless of the negative impact on my neighbor. Selfishness distorts self interest and causes us to lose our soul. We will explore the various forms this perversion of self interest takes in regard to our wealth more in Chapter 2, but Jesus adds clarity to the broader discussion of wealth in our lives.

The Hard Sayings of Jesus

It is clear that Jesus warned us against the dangers of prosperity in many of His teachings. To those of us that work in the world where profit is valued and where we judge economic success in terms of bottom line growth some of Jesus' teachings can make us squirm. Here is a sample:

"A man's life does not consist in the abundance of his possessions." Luke 12:15

"It is easier for a camel to go through the eye of a needle than for a rich man to enter the kingdom of God." Matt 19:24

"How hard it is for those who have riches to enter the kingdom of God." Luke 18:24

Attitude Readjustment: Embracing the Goodness of Wealth

"Sell all that you have and distribute to the poor...and come follow me." Luke 18:22

"Woe to you that are rich." Luke 6:24

These passages, especially read in the context of the Old Testament, make it clear that the accumulation of wealth was a major concern for Jesus.

Hmmm. If we stopped with those verses it would be very compelling to agree that Jesus wants us to simply live in poverty. However, Jesus' views on wealth are not as simplistic and reductionist as some would have us believe. Consider, for example, some of the parables: The Unjust Steward (Luke 16:1-13), The Parable of the Talents (Matt 25:14-30) or The Parable of the Minas (Luke 19: 11-27). While teaching spiritual principles, all of these parables are concerned with the proper management of resources and the virtue of growing them to produce more. Those that were resourceful and produced wealth were applauded and those that failed were rebuked. Furthermore, Jesus had no problem accepting the hospitality of the rich (Luke 11:37, Luke 14:1, Luke 5:29), or using their resources (Mark 3:9, Luke 8:3). Contrary to what many may believe, he also never made a rule that the rich should sell all they possess as shown in the story of Zaccheus (Luke 19:1-10) who was very rich, but was applauded by Jesus even though he did not give away all his wealth. Additionally, Jesus' teaching that he came not to abolish the law (Matt 5:17) would include the eighth commandment, "Thou shalt not steal." This is the fundamental tenet that actually establishes the right to private property, because it would not be necessary if God did not intend for us to own anything!

An overwhelming concept taught in both the Old and New Testaments is that we are to be good stewards of whatever we have been entrusted with. The objective of the steward is to protect and grow the master's resources. We see this in the very first verses of the Bible in what is sometimes called the "first great commission." We are to be fruitful and increase in number, fill the earth and subdue it (Gen 1:28) and in God's charge to cultivate the ground. (Gen 2:23)

How do we reconcile these seemingly incongruent statements? I believe the unifying principle here is that Jesus was going about establishing a kingdom that was spiritual and not secular. The essence of His teaching was dealing with man's attempt to be autonomous of God in all of life, including wealth. Wealth can be used for enjoyment, recognizing it as a gift from God, or it can lead us to forget our need of God. Therefore it makes sense that it was a fertile topic for Jesus to use to uncover the hidden idols in the lives of many that he met.

When Jesus talks about money we should not seek to understand it in the context of some grand political program for economic reform, but rather in terms of our personal spiritual destiny. Jesus knew that the way we handle money, think about money and use money was a window into our relationship with God- in fact into our very soul. I believe there are at least five key principles we can embrace from Jesus' teaching on money:

1. There is nothing inherently redemptive about poverty or sinful about accumulating wealth. Rather, how we think about money should be used as a key indicator about our relationship with God. If we are looking to money to save us or to feed our ego, Jesus would have harsh words for us about our false idol. Similarly, if we look to our poverty as a redeeming virtue, we mistake Jesus' teaching on stewardship and growing whatever talents we have been given.
2. Jesus doesn't even hint that earning money by working in a business is intrinsically wrong. Jesus himself was involved in

a trade for most of his life as a carpenter. The rich fool was made an example (Luke 12:17-21) not for his success at generating wealth, but because his life is focused on glorifying himself and not God.
3. Jesus taught that we are stewards for God of whatever we have been given, both spiritually and physically. God gives us whatever we possess and we are expected to make it grow and prosper. (Luke 16:11). This teaching of Jesus is rooted in the Old Testament command to mankind to "subdue and rule" the earth (Gen 1:28). We are stewards of God's earth and are to "till and keep it" for God. (Gen 2:15)
4. Jesus clearly understood and taught that with wealth there can come spiritual temptations to idolize our money in place of reliance on God. If we forget that we are just stewards with the task of overseeing the wealth God has entrusted us with, we can develop a spirit of self-reliance that makes our heart grow cold towards God.
5. Concern for the poor must be part of kingdom work, but should not extinguish the spirit of celebration and delight that should be a characteristic of Christian communities. Jesus identified with and cared deeply about the poor, but also came eating and drinking. We would do well to integrate celebration alongside ministry to the poor.

All this analysis of Jesus' view of wealth is instructive for our inner spiritual growth, but he wasn't trying to teach a course on economics. To understand the natural expression of a Christian worldview in economics, it is instructive to look at how the teachings of the Bible over the centuries led to building wealth and alleviating the brokenness we find in poverty and suffering.

Recapturing a Christian View of Wealth through Lessons of History

When Martin Luther started the fire that changed the world by posting his ninety-five theses in 1517, he was actually addressing monetary issues. He strongly disputed the claim that freedom from punishment for sin could be purchased. While his protest over buying forgiveness is a well-known fact, what is sometimes forgotten about the Reformation is the tremendous creation of wealth it sparked over time as discussed in the book *The Protestant Ethic and the Spirit of Capitalism*.[xi] This book has been cited as one of the four most important sociological works of the 20th century due to the revelation of the connection between religious beliefs and commerce.[xii] Biblical truths were rediscovered regarding the comprehensive nature of redemption in all of life, including wealth. The life of business, for example, was regarded as dangerous to the soul prior to the Reformation, but it acquired a new sanctity afterward. Monastic life was no longer seen to be the spiritual life of the most holy, but life in the marketplace was seen as the preferred place to best honor God through godly example. Labor was transformed as not merely an economic necessity, but as a spiritual end. There was no longer a conflict seen between money-making and piety, rather, gradually they became allies. Ministers began to teach economic virtues that their flock should practice as their duty to Christ including diligence and thrift. Being productive in a calling and the pursuit of wealth was taught to be not merely an advantage, but a duty. Giving money to the church and the poor was still appropriate, but building capital for businesses and other productive enterprises was also honoring to God because all of life was under his Lordship. By following these principles--the spirit of capitalism--wealth was created and poverty alleviated. The pursuit of riches, which had once been feared as the enemy of religion, became compatible with belief within safeguards of biblical law. John Wesley, an English preacher in the 18th century, coined the phrase that sums up much of the Reformation and biblical teaching on wealth: "Make all you can, save all you can, give all you can."[xiii]

However, in the 20th century, a portion of the Evangelical church had gradually retreated from the Reformation's comprehensive understanding of the kingdom of God and truncated the gospel to focus primarily on evangelism to save souls. The Great Commission was reduced to a pietistic gospel primarily concerned with attending church when the doors were open, avoiding alcohol, drugs and sexual immorality rather than one that made disciples of all nations in all areas of life. The primary concern of many churches became soul winning before the rapture took us off this earth to the neglect of engaging the culture in areas such as building businesses. A popular radio preacher in the 1950's, J. Vernon McGee, created the rhetorical question, "Are you polishing brass on a sinking ship?" to scare Christians away from works of charity and cultural improvement.[xiv] Unfortunately, the church's teaching on money began once again to resemble the pre-reformation teaching that giving to the church is the best use for excess money. Investing in this world was seen as useless as polishing brass on the Titanic.

The church has awakened in recent years to the need to be on the front lines of poverty alleviation as shown in the popularity of books like *When Helping Hurts*.[xv] But, the strongest voices of the poverty fighting power of capitalism have come from outside the church. For example, rock star Bono from U2 has spent a great deal of time and energy fighting world poverty, and has articulated an enlightened view that businesses are the most effective soldiers in this war: "Aid is just a stopgap. Commerce (and) entrepreneurial capitalism takes more people out of poverty than aid. We need Africa to become an economic powerhouse."[xvi]

John Mackey, a former co-op/commune dweller and counterculture movement member of the 60's and 70's recounts his conversion to free enterprise capitalism in the book *Conscious Capitalism.*[xvii] As he became an entrepreneur promoting healthy eating because he could do it more efficiently than the co-op's, he came to appreciate the power of a business with a noble purpose to create prosperity for many. Mr. Mackey, now an advocate for capitalism and co-CEO of Whole Foods Markets, recounts in the book the unprecedented progress of the last 200 years because of free-enterprise capitalism. He points out some interesting facts including 83 percent of the world's population lived in extreme poverty (defined as less than $1 a day) 200 years ago versus 16 percent today.[xviii] Also in just the past forty years, the percentage of undernourished people in the world has dropped from 26 percent to 13 percent.[xix] He is an evangelist for the idea that for-profit business is a powerful instrument for good.

The connection between Christianity as taught by the Reformation churches and prosperity has not gone unnoticed. Some scholars think that China, for example, is more open to Christianity because they see the connection between economic progress and faith.[xx] The economic implications of religious beliefs and prosperity that Max Weber first pointed out in the early 20th century are naturally attractive to pragmatic policy makers. However, to adopt a Christian economic worldview in order to become prosperous is getting the cart before the horse. The fully orbed Christian worldview of Capitalism can only flourish in the long run with hearts changed by grace. The pitfalls of pursuing money without the constraints of Christian charity are the subject of our next chapter. Nevertheless, the Capitalistic economic system that the Reformation produced created an environment that has made great strides in Christian goals of creating prosperity and a corresponding reduction in poverty.

Summary

Christians, and even many business people, are handicapped in reaching their potential and from gaining peace with their finances because of moral confusion about money. No one can confidently move forward in saving more, building a business or even enjoying the blessings of money when conflicted about the morality of wealth. The Bible and the truths of the Reformation, when properly understood, provide a firm foundation to appreciate that God created money to be good for our enjoyment and use. It is a tool to live a life of productivity and celebration as we grow in His Kingdom. However, a Christian worldview also believes that this world has become corrupted because of the fall of man. We move into the next chapter to explore the impact of the fall on money.

(For more reading on the topics of this chapter I would recommend *The Creation of Wealth*,[xxi] which I read many years ago and have drawn on in writing this chapter because it made my role as a Christian in the marketplace much clearer through the years. Other recommendations can be found at smartmoneywithpurpose.com.)

Discussion Questions

1. What is your view of the purpose of and accumulation of wealth? Where did your beliefs about money come from? How do your beliefs compare to what is taught in the Bible?
2. What did you think of the opening story about the man who doesn't use money? Did you react emotionally? Why?
3. Have you considered the plight of the billions of humans in developing countries that live in abject poverty? What has been your response to this fact?
4. Do you agree or disagree with the utilitarian ethic of spending money only in a way that maximizes happiness and reduces suffering of the most people? What philosophy did Jesus operate under? What can we learn from his example?
5. Do you believe secular callings to build businesses are as sacred in God's eyes as calls to the ministry? Why or why not? How do your beliefs impact your view of what you do each day for work?
6. Are you comfortable with the idea that it's okay to want more money? How do we safeguard this desire to keep it from turning into greed?
7. How would you summarize Jesus' teaching on money?

CHAPTER 2

The Deceitfulness of Money

Rub-a-dub-dub,
Three men in a tub;
And who do you think they be?

The butcher, the baker,
The candlestick-maker;
Turn 'em out, knaves all three!

Halliwell, The Nursery Rhymes of England (1846)

The one who received the seed that fell
among the thorns is the man who hears the word,
but the worries of this life and the deceitfulness of
wealth choke it, making it unfruitful.
                                    Matthew 13:22

He who works his land will have abundant food, but the
one who chases fantasies will have his fill of poverty.
                                    Proverbs 28:19

When the crash of the U.S. stock market occurred in 2008 the financial system teetered on the brink of financial collapse. Bankers like me felt helpless, powerless to predict what financial pillar was going to fall next. The news pundits were kept very busy pointing fingers at the likely suspects for the cause of the crises and the ensuing Great Recession. Everyone seems to have taken some blame including the two political parties, the Federal Reserve, Wall Street executives and lax regulators. We could even cite misguided legislation. In hindsight we know that no good came from social goals set by giving incentives to many to own a home when they did not have the means to pay the loan back. While all this may have had a role to play in this economic disaster, what has not been addressed are the spiritual roots of the crises. My three friends' experience goes beneath the headlines and looks closer at the heart of the issue that enabled the house of cards to be built.

The Butcher, the Baker, the Candlestick Maker

Mr. Butcher was single and in his late 20's. He didn't make a lot of money, but he knew that he was where God wanted him because he enjoyed his work and his customers praised him for his skillful meat cuts. He lived a frugal life, but was able to enjoy it without a lot of money because he became friends with many of his customers like Mr. Baker who shared his passion for the outdoors, good wine, great bread and deep conversation.

One day Mr. Baker told Mr. Butcher, "I've quit my job at the bakery and I'm going to start earning some real dough by flipping houses that I can sell at a huge profit."

At first Mr. Butcher thought he was crazy. How can he give up a calling that is perfect for him to pursue something he knows next to nothing about? But then Mr. Baker sold his first house and he took Mr. Butcher out to their favorite restaurant to celebrate.

The Deceitfulness of Money

Mr. Butcher was about to object when Mr. Baker ordered the most expensive Pinot Noir on the wine list, but Mr. Baker cut him off by saying, "I just made $33,000 on the house deal and you're not going to stop me from celebrating the biggest paycheck of my life are you?"

Suddenly Mr. Baker didn't seem quite so crazy anymore. And then Mr. Baker got a loan to buy two more homes and they, too, sold quickly at a nice profit. Mr. Baker was on a roll and poor Mr. Butcher was getting left behind. The butcher business suddenly wasn't looking so attractive anymore. He wondered if he could get in on the action too.

The next day Mr. Butcher called Mr. Baker and asked him if he could teach him how to get in on this housing boom. Mr. Baker said, "I'd be happy to help you get rich. You need to do two things. First, I'll loan you my copy of the book I learned it all in called "Flippin' houses for Knaves," and then I'll introduce you to my loan officer, Mr. Candlestick-maker. He'll get you the money you need to start flippin' away. What you need to know is that there has never been a time in our nation's history when house prices have gone down. My realtor, Ms. Rose Colored, says housing prices always go up 10% a year around here so the profit is guaranteed. She'll teach you about the magic of leverage!"

Mr. Butcher said, "Hey, I think I know Mr. Candlestick-maker. He buys some meat from me, but I thought he was in the lighting business!"

"Well, you're right, he used to be in that business, but the problem was that he couldn't make any serious money at it. He watched a late night commercial on becoming a mortgage broker, took a two day course and now he's doing really well for himself. I guess there are big commissions for those bankers in booking as many loans as they can get."

So the next day Mr. Butcher closed his shop early and went to see Mr. Candlestick-maker. "Sir, I've read the "Flippin houses for Knaves" book as training and I'd like to get one of those mortgage loans so I can flip a house I've found, but I'm afraid I won't qualify for a loan." Mr. Butcher said.

"How much are you going to need," asked Mr. Candlestick-maker?

"Well, the house is on the market for $500,000 so I guess that's what I'll need. I make around $30,000 a year and I wasn't sure if I'd qualify." said Mr. Butcher.

"Qualify, small-e-fy, don't you worry about that Mr. Butcher. We'll get you in that deal one way or another because I want you to be rich just like me from all the commissions I'm making these days. We'll just put down on your application that you make $150,000 out of that butcher shop you run. They never check to see if it's true and you'll have flipped this baby in no time anyway at a big profit so no harm will be done by the little white lie. But first we need to engage the *Whatever You Need* appraisal company to get that baby valued at $600,000 for the loan underwriting."

"Well, that sounds reasonable," said Mr. Butcher…

Post Mortem

And so Mr. Butcher got his loan and soon made a handsome profit on his house. Like Mr. Baker, he quit his job as a butcher and began to build his inventory of houses making great profit… until he didn't. When the music stopped and house prices quit going up, Mr. Butcher and Mr. Baker had several million dollars in loans that could not be repaid. They went through bankruptcy and financial ruin. Both have now returned to their original calling. Mr. Candlestick-maker's mortgage company went bankrupt and he is now being investigated by the FBI for mortgage fraud on loan applications.

How Money Deceives Us

All of us know some version of people like these three who stumbled badly in the Great Recession because of their greed and pursuit of money outside the bounds of their calling and expertise. However, if we're honest with ourselves, we know that we too are easily captured by money's seductive power. We are all capable of doing dumb things when the thrill of quick riches is waived in front of us. I once convinced myself in the late 1990's that I was an expert tech stock picker. After gaining some quick profits and subscribing to a technology investment newsletter, I was suddenly an expert in computer chips and telecommunications. As in the case of our three friends above, I learned when the market crashed in 2000 and 2001 that I wasn't as smart as I thought I was and the real motive--quick easy profits-- was revealed as my own costly penalty for getting snared in money's deceit.

But how does money deceive us exactly? Why is it a potential hindrance to our spiritual health? In Matthew 13:22 Jesus says, "The one who received the seed that fell among the thorns is the man who hears the word, but the worries of this life and the deceitfulness of wealth choke it, making it unfruitful." Jesus' warning is stark: If you let money deceive you, it can choke out the power of God's kingdom in your life! I'm not sure how Jesus could have spoken more sternly. We need to understand the power that money can exert. How can a Christian effectively counterpunch against such a powerful force?

Let's look closely at the two parts to Jesus' explanation in this passage. I believe he linked them intentionally because they fit like a hand in a glove. First, "the worries of this life" are all too familiar to us. We worry if we will be able to put our kids through college, if we will have enough money to pay the bills, if we will run out of money in retirement, or even be able to afford health care. In both big issues and small, we wonder if we will have enough money to get everything done.

Worries are always entering our mind, but it's like mixing gas and fire when we combine our worries with the deceitfulness of wealth. Wealth seems like the perfect answer to our worries. All these problems we fret about seem easily solved if only we had more money. The more money we make, the more secure our future seems. So logically we look to acquire more wealth to ease our worried minds instead of trusting God for our security. Our consumer culture reinforces this character weakness by constantly bombarding us with more products and services required to achieve happiness. We enjoy so much prosperity that we see money as the solution to almost any problem we face. In fact, in Biblical language, lusting after wealth becomes an idol because it turns us away from the only thing that has the real power to change our hearts and give us contentment and freedom from worry in this world. The Apostle Paul echoes Jesus' warning about money's ability to turn us away from the true God in Colossians 3:5, "…greed, which is idolatry."

There are biblical measures we might use to determine if we desire more money in an appropriate way as discussed in chapter one, or if we have tipped over into something unhealthy to our soul. Proverbs 28:19 is instructive, "He who works his land will have abundant food, but the one who chases fantasies will have his fill of poverty." If our desire for more money is equivalent to chasing fantasies that are clearly outside of our own unique gifts (working our own land) in order to get rich quick, we have in all likelihood gone over the line. Similarly, "dishonest money dwindles away, but whoever gathers money little by little makes it grow" (Pr. 13:11) is a good test. If our actions to gain more money are unethical and don't incorporate the command to "love our neighbor," or if we are impatient in wanting to get rich, we have also crossed a line into greed and idolatry. You might say the butcher in the opening story who decided to become a house flipping, multi-millionaire really fast, instead of growing rich slowly in his calling, would be a good example of one who failed these tests.

Envy of other peoples' wealth is another powerful force of deception that the Bible addresses. "A heart at peace gives life to the body, but envy rots the bones."(Pr 14:30) Politicians exploit this human frailty because they know they can obtain votes by appealing to something inside of us that wants to think we are being cheated because of others' success. Considerable emphasis on "income inequality" in recent years in the political circles inflames the problem. We have to be careful with this topic because in some cultures the poor are oppressed by the rich. However, even a cursory review of American economic history shows how misguided this analysis is in our country. When World War II ended, income and wealth inequalities were narrower than they've been at anytime in the past century.[xxii] However, middle-class Americans did not have smartphones, air conditioning, and access to cheap airfare or the wide variety of affordable pills to treat multiple medical conditions to name just a few differences during that time of relative income equality. Personally, I would much rather have some income inequality, but access to all the services that have been created by tremendous wealth creation, than a situation where we are all equally in misery. But the real point is not political, but spiritual. Envy of others' wealth may feel good for a time, but in the end it rots the bones. We would be wise to guard our hearts against this sin and be mindful of attempts by others to manipulate us by exploiting this human weakness.

Money deceives us in other ways too. We set a "number" that we must get to before we can retire or move on to a second act God may be calling us to serve in. Inevitably, however, we find that once we attain it, we instead keep salting away more money and move our "number" ever higher. My industry does all it can to reinforce this continual striving for more by warning of all the ways we can run out of money once we're past our peak years. However, no one mentions in the advertisements that the more money we keep in retirement accounts, the more fees are collected by asset managers. The point is that money is a cruel taskmaster of our lives when we believe it has the power of God to meet our needs.

Money and Happiness

Despite advertisers' best efforts to convince us, money as an idol will not solve our problems or make us happy. In the last 35 years researchers have studied happiness as an academic discipline including the impact of sudden wealth gains. For example, one foundational study on happiness in 1978 reported in the *Journal of Personality and Social Psychology* compared winners of the Illinois lottery with victims of devastating accidents that had been left with some paralysis.[xxiii] The lottery winners clearly rated the initial exhilaration of winning as a highly positive experience, but over time the winners were not considered happier than the victims of tragic accidents. In fact, the accident victims even had a more positive outlook for the future regarding their expectation of future happiness.

Other studies have concluded that happiness does increase when those living below the poverty level gain additional income. If you aren't feeding your children and you gain new wealth that allows you to give proper nourishment to your family, you will be happier, for example. However, as the amount of income grows over a base of providing for basic needs, the level of happiness levels off and actually may begin to decline.[xxiv] One theory suggests that we live our lives on a "hedonic treadmill."[xxv] This theory holds that we quickly adjust to improved status and as soon as we reach one level of economic status such as a new car or a new iPhone toy, our expectations quickly ramp up looking for the next thrill. In the end, we are left no happier than we were before we acquired the new wealth. This should not be a surprise to a Christian who has read Jesus' words that "life does not consist in the abundance of his possessions." (Luke 12:15)

Researchers have also found that our level of happiness is tied to our perception of the wealth of those around us.[xxvi] If we have a close friend who has more wealth than we do, we tend to think of him or her as "the wealthy" and ourselves as middle class even though the poorest American lives better than most of the world. In other words, focusing on our neighbor's wealth can deceive us into believing we are below average and in need of more stuff to be happy. Jealous envy steals our joy.

But happiness is the not the primary goal of the Christian. As one Reformation Catechism stated in the 1550's, the chief end of man is "to glorify God and enjoy him forever."[xxvii] So what is the best way to do that with our money?

The Solution to the Problem

Many unhelpful teachings on wealth and poverty circulate through various branches of the church. An endless number of perspectives exist, but there are three major schools on what the Bible teaches about wealth. Two are very dangerous to your soul, but there is a third way that is consistent with living a productive, joyful and Kingdom-focused life.

The first is poverty or liberation theology which has a low view of anything of this world, especially man's pursuit of money. It rejects materialism and has a strong interest in helping the poor overcome rich oppressors. Like the other views, it can point to verses in the Bible that seem to support it's suppositions. However, it does not represent a balanced view of the Bible's teaching on wealth. Poverty does not equal righteousness. The poor can be just as lustful for wealth as rich people. Furthermore, poverty theology provides no basis for reclaiming our lost world and healing relationships that lead to industriousness and eventual wealth creation. It leaves us in a cycle of poverty that makes it wrong to ever break out of it. Liberation theology ultimately ostracizes those who break out of the poverty ghetto, assuming that they only did it by oppressing others or failing to give away what they possess.

The polar opposite of poverty theology could be called prosperity theology which also attempts to base its teaching on certain Scriptures, but is equally misplaced in understanding the whole teaching of Christianity. In short, this position argues that if we will believe and obey, God is bound by His own laws to make us rich. It teaches that you create a binding contract with God in which he is bound to bless you. While it's true that obedient Christians generally prosper because they lead a life of fidelity, frugality and hard work, God also knows our weaknesses and refines us at times with trials that include suffering and financial hardship. Following God does not guarantee riches.

While both of these extreme views contain elements of truth, the Bible does provide a more unifying theme that is best called "stewardship theology." The concepts of stewardship avoid the mistakes of the other views of wealth and give us the correct framework to understand how we can best glorify God with our wealth, whatever our station in life might be.

In short, stewardship theology is a powerful and life-changing belief that we relinquish ownership of all our earthly possessions. Ps 24:1 teaches that God owns the world and by adopting this mindset we acknowledge that God is the owner of all that we have, but we are given the high charge of managing His resources for Him. The parable of the talents in Matthew 25:14-30 illustrates this principle. The Master went on a journey and left his three servants with some money. The first servant was given five bags of gold, the second was given two bags and the third was given one. The master entrusted them with what he thought they were capable of handling. The first two servants immediately went out and invested the money and doubled it. The third servant buried his treasure in fear and therefore it did not grow in value. When the master returned the first two servants were praised for their excellent stewardship and rewarded with even more money to oversee. The third servant was severely chastised and punished for being a poor steward and not making the money grow. This parable is worthy of frequent meditation to remind us that we have all been given resources, some few and some many. But whether rich or poor, God expects us to be putting them to use to increase their value. This applies to spiritual gifts, but it can also include our wealth. It is an incredibly freeing philosophy for managing our money, but also one that will create wealth and alleviate poverty through an infinite variety of individual callings.

Examples of Putting Stewardship Theology into Practice

Let's consider how two people in different circumstances who are equally committed to living a life of good stewardship might make different decisions with their wealth, but both would be praise worthy.

First, let's look at a man I have admired for his business accomplishments named Sam Walton. Sam built the Wal-Mart franchise starting from a single store in Arkansas into one of the largest and most successful corporations in the world employing about 2.2 million people. While criticized by some for various reasons, let's put aside that critique for now, for the sake of this illustration. Assume that a study on Wal-Mart's impact is accurate that reported the company brought about a reduction in the prices of consumer goods equal to $895 per person between 1985 and 2004. This savings represented $2,329 per household.[xxviii]

So in effect, Wal-Mart has a tremendous impact on reducing the cost of necessities to the poor and middle class, or anyone who shops. To add an extra $2,329 per household would be a major accomplishment for any charitable agency looking to help the poor. In fact, you could argue that Sam Walton was one way God has answered our prayer to "give us this day our daily bread" because we have more disposable income because of him. One could argue that Sam Walton's life work, in addition to making him and his shareholders wealthy, also was a major poverty fighter.

But let's imagine back to the day Sam started the first Wal-Mart store. It must have been very successful and I assume he could have had a happy, productive life as a one-store merchant his whole life. It's my understanding that Sam was a churchgoer and I'm sure he could have looked at his meager wealth in the beginning and decided to contribute all the excess to the local church instead of reinvesting to grow his business. However, I suspect his calling focused his time, treasure and talents on building the company. I don't know how much Sam gave to charity in those early days, but the Bible gives us ample reason to believe that we should always be giving at least 10% of our increase to fund churches and other charities. But the question we all face is where the excess over that amount should be put. He not only chose to put everything he had into growing the business, but took on debt too. Was this wise stewardship? I think it was. In fact it would have been poor stewardship if he had funneled his excess into the church at that point in his life and missed his calling to build a powerful, low-cost retail enterprise. A powerful theme of Scripture is that Jesus is actively sustaining and redeeming not just the religious systems in which humans live, but also the economic and political realms. (Colossians 1: 16-17) You see, when we adopt a Christian worldview that looks at all of life as sacred and under the dominion of God, it is also a legitimate use of our wealth to build businesses or other institutions that can be under the Lordship of Christ and used by him to achieve his purposes.

In contrast, let's look at a college professor the same age as Sam was when he started his first store. She has a secure pension she is building, only a small mortgage and is able to save about 30% of her income a year because of her frugal lifestyle. I'll call her Rachel. She hears about the charitable work going on in an orphanage in India and is moved by it. As a steward of God's wealth she may ask herself if she should continue to pile up more wealth in her mutual funds or put this excess to work in the orphanage home. She doesn't have a need for more capital funding to achieve her purpose in life and believes that the orphanage is the best Kingdom building use for her excess cash flow. She commits to giving away 30% of her income for the rest of her working life. She passionately tells others about the orphanage and convinces them to fly to India on occasion to help with the work and to raise more money. This generous support from her and her friends allows the orphanage to expand and grow so they can house an additional 30 children. Those children grow up and become productive members of society because of her generosity and calling to make a difference in their lives. What a fantastic legacy she is leaving because she decided to invest her time and money in needy children.

Was either person wrong in their decision? Sam reinvested his excess cash flow into his growing business and Rachel put her funds in the orphanage. Both were already giving 10% of their increase to a church, but took totally different paths with the excess over that amount. They took separate paths in faith out of a conviction that they were being wise stewards and both extended God's kingdom in different ways. Not many pastors or even Christian financial planners think about the Kingdom in this all encompassing way. But when we give up all we own and become a steward of what God has given us, it frees us from money's deceit and we see the world in a new way. We have great freedom in how to manage God's resources as long as we are making them multiply.

These two people could represent the two wise stewards in the parable of the talents in Matthew 25 that were commended by the Master, but I would be remiss if I did not discuss the third steward who buried the money he was given. He did not make it multiply because he was too fearful to take any risks and/or too lazy to be productive. This guy represents a large percentage of our population who only has the ambition to sit on the couch, watch TV and be a really smart sports fan. He might be a big buyer of lottery tickets as a way to dream about hitting it big, but his self-absorbed life ends up contributing little to the world. He will never make a difference for the Kingdom of God living life this way!

Looking at Stewardship in Reverse

How can you tell if you have really given all your worldly wealth to God and are managing His wealth as a wise steward? A great test might be to imagine what expectations you would have if you were suddenly disabled in a traffic accident and were unable to manage your money. Let's assume you received a $3,000,000 settlement from the insurance company that you turned over to the trust department of First National Bank and Trust Company to manage on your behalf.

What would you think if the trust officer suddenly traded in his 10 year old Chrysler Sebring for a brand new Porsche? When you asked him about it, he just said, "Well since you gave me that $3,000,000 to manage I thought you would want me to travel around managing your money in style." And then you notice that he has made some reckless investments in penny stocks and his explanation is, "You've got plenty where that came from so I just thought we'd be a little reckless and gamble a bit on these stocks."

My guess is that you would fire this trust officer very quickly. However, when we are blessed with wealth do we find that we similarly lose our discipline with God's money? Do we suddenly think we have enough to relax and splurge on some luxuries? Quit working? Or gamble a bit in the stock market because if we lose the money, it's not that big of a deal? Of course, it's not a perfect analogy because God is a lot more loving to us than we would be to the hapless trust officer. He does indeed want us to enjoy the good things he has given us in proportion to our position in life. However, we should always keep in mind that it is his wealth that we are managing and treat every penny with the respect we would want a steward to have for our money. We should never find ourselves buying into the notion that we might as well spend our wealth because we can't take it with us. Rather, as we will discuss in chapter 10, we should aim for leaving an inheritance as an important part of stewardship of God's wealth.

Summary

The financial crises that led to the Great Recession has provided an apt laboratory to investigate the spiritual decay behind our economic downfall. If we are honest, we will see that we too are easily deceived by the allure of quick riches. Empirical research in recent years has confirmed what the Bible has taught for thousands of years: we do not find happiness in more and more money. The solution to protecting us from this deceit is to give up our rights to our wealth and consider ourselves stewards of God's wealth. This powerful and radical idea will transform our lives as we seek to multiply the value of the gifts we have been given whether they are monetary or spiritual.

Discussion Questions

1. How can wealth be deceitful? How has it deceived you?
2. What are the possible economic implications when we make decisions based on being blinded by wealth's deceitfulness? The spiritual implications?
3. How does the deceitfulness of wealth choke out the gospel as Jesus warned about in Matt 13:22?
4. What is the relationship of money and happiness in your life? Is the reality different than the dream about how much happiness more money will bring?
5. Why do you think many in the history of the church have adopted a view of wealth called "poverty theology?" What are its strengths? Weaknesses?
6. What is good about "prosperity theology?" What are its strengths? Weaknesses?
7. What are the strengths and weaknesses of "stewardship theology"? If you adopted this view, how would it change the way you manage your finances?

CHAPTER 3

The Foundation: Putting the Power of Purpose in Your Financial Plan

"The two most important days of your life are the day you were born…and the day you find out why."
Mark Twain

"We are His workmanship created in Christ Jesus to do good works".
Eph 2:10

For the past several years, I have been counseling with a close friend of mine about his career. He had become a successful accountant after graduating from college six years earlier. But as he approached turning 30 years old he was becoming convinced that he was being called to an entrepreneurial life. However, it's not an easy thing to walk away from the comforts of a big corporate job. While job security is always at risk because of periodic downsizings, the money is good, the benefits are great and the quality of people he associated with was excellent. As we worked through a framework for making this decision, it became clear that it was the right decision for him. However, what I did not expect was that when he finally pulled the trigger and announced that he was leaving he gained "rock star" status among his co-workers! He was bombarded with lunch requests to learn how he was going to go on his own. They wanted out too! The keen interest others had in leaving a highly respected international company enlightened me about the passion that exists in the corporate world for finding more meaningful work. But a decision like this has huge financial implications that need to be thought through carefully.

This topic is so hot that it seems odd to me that the financial planning industry does not emphasize it more. I believe a chapter on finding your life purpose in a book about managing money is crucial. Many money managers are required to spend a few minutes asking you about your life goals for compliance purposes. However, it should not be just a perfunctory exercise; it is foundational for true success with money to develop a financial plan that is in sync with our hoped for destiny. The cornerstone for any discussion about personal finances is to find answers to the hard questions of who you are and what God put you on this earth to accomplish.

In my counseling I have found individuals or couples will come to me for advice on a particular financial problem such as not being able to live within their means. Usually they are surprised when I begin our discussion probing them on their calling in life instead of their budget. My questions are unexpected and sometimes uncomfortable, but most folks quickly see the wisdom of ordering their finances around a larger purpose in life. In fact, when we have a clear understanding of how we can specifically "glorify God and enjoy Him forever," then we can develop a laser-focused financial plan and avoid common pitfalls, both spiritual and practical, that derail those with unfocused aspirations. We'll get to the financial side, but first let's start by going back again to the spiritual roots of our purpose in life.

The Christian and His Calling

The Bible is clear that we are to be on guard against the love of money, but as a general rule, those living a Christian life in obedience to Christ become wealthy. Why? It is one of Christianity's most fascinating paradoxes. One reason Christians are generally successful in life is because of the belief that all lawful callings, not just those in the church, are equally acceptable in the eyes of God. The baker, Luther taught, was used by God to answer the prayer, "Give us this day our daily bread," thereby sanctifying his daily work.[xxix] It was not just the priest that was given a holy calling, but all of life is an act of worship. Therefore the Christian has great motivation to perform her work with excellence, because it is an act of worship.

Cotton Mather was a Colonial preacher in the 18th century that brought this message to America. His sermon, "A Christian at His Calling"[xxx] preached in 1701 is still instructive for us today in our world of lost souls trying to find a purpose for living. He thundered to his flock, "Every Christian should have a calling. That is to say, there should be some special business...wherein a Christian should for the most part spend the most of his time; and this, that so he may glorify God...But it is not lawful for a Christian ordinarily to live without some calling or another...but how can a man reasonably look for the help of other men, if he be not in some calling helpful to other men?" And he also spoke relevant words to those who can seemingly never find satisfaction in a job, "It is the singular favor of God, unto a man, that he can attend his occupation with contentment and satisfaction. That one man has a spirit formed and fitted for one occupation, and another man for another, this is from the operation of God..."

We continue our discussion of finances with a discussion of "purpose in life" because if we get that wrong we will not get our finances aligned with who we are meant to be. The spiritual and the physical sides of our life should be synchronized. If we find our sweet spot, we are able to accomplish great things because there is a passion behind our effort that is rooted in the morality of our work. If we do not, in a consumerist culture such as ours, the default option will usually be accumulating more money and more things and failing to live intentionally. Or, in some with a more timid or pessimistic disposition, fear is likely to take over when there is a vacuum without a sense of a divine calling. Instead of an aggressive, dominion outlook on life with a purpose, they tend to become excessive savers, hoarding any excess that can be accumulated in fear of the unknown calamity that might overtake them. However, if we understand our purpose in life, if we know our Lord and that he "has plans for us...plans to prosper us and not to harm us, plans to give us hope and a future," (Jeremiah 29:11) then we approach life with a different attitude. A purpose focused life can accomplish great things, and a side benefit is the order and shalom it can bring into our financial lives.

But what is purpose? Purpose can be defined simply as a confidence that our life and our place in the world truly matters. It's a belief that we contribute something special to others which God has prepared for us to do. And if our purpose is authentic enough, it affects us deeply and we align all areas of our life around that calling. Most who live in the knowledge of a calling will simplify their lives and eliminate clutter to pursue it. Living on less may occur, but it doesn't seem like depravation when we are focused. Rather, it becomes joyful living at its best.

Three Friends and Their Life Purpose

Let me tell you about three of my friends who each have a different foundation, or lack of one, for what drives their relationship with money.

First, you'll probably recognize folks like Don and Carol. They were caught up in the real estate frenzy that convinced them that bigger is better and that it was an American right to have your house increase in value each year. They bought a million dollar house in Arizona with a lot of easy-to-obtain debt knowing that it would appreciate and they could sell it in a few years at a big profit when they were ready to retire. When things started to go south, they had an offer, but they would have had to take a hit close to $100,000. While they could afford it, they *knew* the market would come back and so they bet their future on it and turned down the offer. Now Carol has health problems and needs to quit her strenuous job but they can't make the payments without her income. The value of their house has fallen precipitously and they can't get a nibble even at a reduced price. Nothing in the market is selling over $400,000. They have a very fine house, but not much of a life. Instead of the house being a blessing, it has become a curse. They believe that in this season of life their purpose should be retiring to less taxing volunteer work and spending more time helping with grandkids, but they feel trapped and wish they had never dreamed of putting all their financial energy into having the million dollar house.

Jenny had a different dream- not one that you or I would probably ever share--she runs a junk yard! One day a few years ago I called on Jenny in the middle of a hot and humid August afternoon. Little did I know how passionate Jenny was about her bunch of, well, junk! After I asked her to tell me about the business we spent the next two hours walking through her empire talking about the pros and cons of the various types of junk that she handled while I loosened my tie, started sweating profusely and wondered why I didn't plan this call on a cooler day. Never again have I lacked appreciation for the old saying that "one man's junk is another's treasure." Jenny doesn't make a lot of money in her line of work, but she loves it. As I've found with many of my entrepreneurial customers, she has found her calling in life. Her objectives are not primarily to maximize wealth, even though Jenny makes a good living, but to allow her to serve customers and fulfill her dream of recycling other people's waste.

Finally, let me tell you about a wise 20-something young man named Albert. Albert was in my Sunday school class a few years ago in Illinois and as we were sharing about financial principles he offered a little of his story. He felt pressured out of high school to attend Bible College from his family. As he went through a semester of this program he began to take out student loans and realized that it was going to take a long time to pay the debt back. More importantly, Albert realized that he was not really sure that he wanted to be a pastor and made a decision to drop out of the school, work to pay off the debt he had accumulated and give more serious thought to what he felt called to do in life. In contrast to the average college student today who graduates with over $29,000 of debt and, many with much more, Albert is debt free and following an intentional path of finding a vocation. Unlike many twenty something young adults today, he chose to not just hang out for four years in college living on student loans.

So could my three friends benefit from a reevaluation of their underlying purpose in life and their financial practices? My experience is that all of us gain remarkable new understanding when we take the opportunity to think through our purpose in life and only then build our financial plan. Advice from Wall Street marketers or green eye shade accountants on Main Street will address tactical matters regarding our money, but not matters of the heart. Don and Carol just feel trapped by their past poor real estate decisions. Exploring their deepest desires to help with grandkids and take on less stressful jobs may open them up to consider more creative financial alternatives to deal with their obligations. They may be able to rent their mansion at a price sufficient to cover their mortgage payment and downsize to an apartment allowing them to accomplish their current life goals. Jenny on the other hand may want to look at expanding her business to grow more efficient in serving others. Finally, Albert has called a time-out and is trying to find God's plan for his life without mortgaging his future options. The bottom line is that all of us could benefit from a friend to help us think through the tough questions of our calling in life and the financial reorientation that will follow. So let's work through this together.

How to find your purpose

You may agree with all I have said so far, but be wondering just what your purpose in life is! And if that isn't complicated enough, I am convinced that it is not something that stays constant for most people. Our purpose can change with the various seasons of life. For young people, purpose may be easier: we get married, have kids and go to work to support our family. Many don't struggle with questions of purpose in these early stages of life. But as you grow older it seems purpose and meaning can absorb more of our thinking. Regardless of our age, we should be thoughtful about it along with the financial implications.

I have struggled with questions of purpose and meaning at various times. I came to a point in 2004 where I found myself going to the self improvement section of bookstores because I was not finding meaning in my work. Unfortunately, I really didn't find a lot of satisfying answers there. There were plenty of ideas on how to achieve goals, but not much that dealt with the more foundational questions of purpose and calling. I had been the CEO of a successful community bank for many years in Illinois and it sold in 1999 to a much larger bank. The new job with the acquiring bank intrigued me for several years, but I began to grow restless and discontent in my regional president role. After many discussions with my wife, I came to realize that I was better suited to running a business rather than being a cog in the corporate hierarchy. About that time I saw an ad in the Wall Street Journal for a CEO position at a community bank in Montana- quite a contrast to Southern Illinois. I had never been to Montana, but flying out and seeing the Rocky Mountains and having the chance to get back to running a community bank made me realize that it was time for a change. Even at 50 years of age with four kids to move with me, it made perfect sense. I became alive again. It was what I was made to do and I have not looked back. However, getting to that point was full of ambiguity and confusion. Here are a few things I have learned that might assist you in your journey to nail this down for a season.

There is no magic dust that we can sprinkle to get the answer to our purpose and calling in life. Some feel called to a specific purpose early in life, but most of us periodically wrestle with our calling. And, many of us go through transitional phases in our lives where we have to reexamine this question even after a season of life where we knew exactly what our purpose in life was. Many stay-at-home mothers, for example, go through this period of uncertainty as their children leave the nest and their identity becomes less certain. I've often thought midlife crises might be better labeled as a crisis of life purpose.

The Foundation: Putting the Power of Purpose in Your Financial Plan

Some financial planners have begun to integrate more questions dealing with heart issues before jumping into the development of a financial plan. I think this is a healthy trend, and I encourage you to do this analysis on your own to help clarify your life purpose. Thoughtful questions such as, "What kind of work would you pursue if every job paid the same amount of money?" can help us strip away the fog created by money to focus on what we really want to do in life. Or, it might help you clarify who you are at your core if you asked yourself if you just inherited ten million dollars, how would you change your life? In other words, what is really important to you in life that you are not now fulfilling? It doesn't really matter which way you ask the questions as long as you spend some time thinking about how your life would change if pursuit of money were not a factor in your decision. Only after you are settled in the answers to questions like these should you then reintroduce the money factor. But, the chemistry of your thinking will have changed at that point. Accumulation of money will no longer be a driving factor in your decision making process; instead the question becomes, how am I going to use money to achieve my purpose in life? Money becomes your servant at that point, a useful tool to help you achieve your God given purpose.

Some highly paid professionals, for example, hate what they do. However, if they never ask themselves penetrating questions such as these they will likely have a default option of working to accumulate more and more money with the hope of exiting their hated profession someday. How sad to work at something you don't enjoy through your most productive years and to settle for a few years at the end of your career doing something you were created to enjoy. I have seen some folks take a different path early in life after looking themselves in the mirror with honest self assessment.

As you think about your responses to these questions, what do you learn about yourself? Are there any changes you are willing to make to accomplish any of the desires you noted? It may be as simple as one friend's decision to save some money for a trip to see her relatives more often, or as life changing as a new career direction. Be open to thinking that is out of your comfort zone.

Practical Suggestions

There are many other resources available to assist us in our quest to come to grips with our purpose in life. I found Max Lucado's book, *Cure for the Common Life, Living in Your Sweet Spot*[xxxi] particularly helpful as I made my transition to Montana. Your source of wisdom and insight may be unique, but here are a few suggestions you might consider in doing the hard work of examining your life for purpose before you attempt to draft your financial plan:

- Ps 32:8 "I will instruct you and teach you in the way you should go." Pray and ask God to show you your purposes(s) in life.
- Ps 37:4 "Delight yourself in the Lord and He will give you the desires of your heart." What do you love to do? What do you do well? Perhaps there is a clue to the maze in your wiring. Delight is a major theme in the Bible as God generally plans for us to be enjoying his creation by expressing our creativity in taking dominion over it. Once we know ourselves, Proverbs 3 tells us what to do: "Trust in the Lord with all your heart and do not lean on your own understanding, in all your ways acknowledge him and he will direct your path."
- Luke 12:15 "…Be on your guard against all kinds of greed; a man's life does not consist in the abundance of his possessions." Investment banking on Wall Street may be the quickest route to riches, but if that is the goal of our life instead of finding our calling then we can be sure it will

The Foundation: Putting the Power of Purpose in Your Financial Plan

bring misery. Test your heart and try to eliminate money from the equation for awhile in assessing where you can be most useful to the kingdom of God.

- Pr 15:22 "Plans fail for lack of counsel, but with many advisers they succeed." What do others think you do well? Find qualified friends that can help you sort out the confusion of choices in life to see what gifts others recognize in you. In addition, there are many professional "life coaches" that are very good at helping us define our purpose and developing plans to achieve it if you have the resources to pay for this assistance.
- Be aware of the way God's purposes for us might change in the different season's of life along with the financial implications:

Age	Purpose Possibilities	Potential Purposeful Financial Goal
0-25	Discover calling/develop talents	Save for college, emergency fund, save for car
20-55	Building business, gaining influence	Insurance, house, pay off debt, savings
55-80	2nd act, elder, politics, serve more	Radical giving, legacy, inheritance, Long term care insurance

- There are many assessment tools available that test and help us discover our passions and identity. Crown Financial Ministries is a Christian organization that offers one such tool called "Career Direct" that has helped many who have struggled with these purpose questions.
- Don't feel obligated to come up with a life purpose that is an adventure. Your particular calling may be as simple as staying in your current job to provide the resources for your family's special needs. The beauty of our world is that everyone is created with some gift or gifts that God will use.

The Four Legged Stool Financial Test for Career Change

So if you have come to a conclusion that you are being called to another type of work, when should you make the leap? It is not an academic question as you will likely be facing multiple financial challenges to make a change from a career in which you have invested significant time and resources. I suggest you consider four things that you can visualize as legs on a stool to determine the wisdom of moving forward. The more legs on the stool that are stable, the more likely your plan will succeed. You may not be able to have all four legs where you would like to have them before making a change, but you should consider each one and the strength of the overall plan.

First, have you lost your passion and sense of call in your current job? If not, you are in a great spot and should continue to develop your skills to be the best that you can be. However, if you find yourself daydreaming at work about doing something different, you may be experiencing the first symptoms of a call to a second act in your life. This can be a very confusing time, but we should learn to embrace the uncertainty as a possible sign of God's calling us to a new ministry.

Second, I don't encourage anyone to simply quit their day job to go pursue a dream without some validation that they will be successful. For example, if you have an idea for a new business, work on it part time for awhile. If you begin to get traction, generating sales and making some money, this is an excellent indicator that you will be even more successful if you were able to pursue it full time. However, without test driving your new career you may end up with some deep regrets.

Third, whether you are single, or especially if you are married and your family depends on your income, I recommend a year of cash be set aside if possible to lessen the financial pressure in the transition year. You will have enough on your plate starting a new venture without having to lay awake at night worrying about where your next meal money is going to come from. A full year of cash may be daunting to accumulate, but you can attack this goal in two ways. First, accumulate all you can in cash, and second reduce your living expenses as much as possible in order to be free to pursue your dream.

Fourth, do you have the endorsement of those close to you? If you're married, I would normally not encourage moving forward without your spouse's encouragement. When adult children have good relationships with their parents, they should use them as valued counselors too. They know you well and many times can offer valued perspective on your strengths and weaknesses. Or if you are in a church community group or similar affiliation that brings you together regularly with others that have an interest in your success, use them to find out their honest assessment of your ability to succeed.

The young man in the opening paragraph of this chapter made sure each of these legs of the stool were tested before he made his decision to jump out of corporate America. For example, he framed an e-mail that he got from one of his bosses asking him to provide an update on a $0.02 transaction. That memo represented to him why he was losing his passion for his job. Such meaningless minutia was not inspiring him. Second, he had worked after hours for more than a year on his idea. By the time he turned in his two week notice he was confident he should be able to make enough for his family to live on if he pursued his opportunities full time. He had also diligently set aside a year of living expenses in a money market account so he felt confident that even if he had a slump, he would have time to recover from it. And finally, he had a diverse group of counselors advising him to move forward. His wonderful wife was encouraging him to make the transition. He had belonged to a church community group for many years and their prayers and encouragement were also behind him. And, his parents told him that they had seen him even as a child demonstrate the entrepreneurial drive and patience for the new career he desired. His parents realize that he may stumble in his new venture because it is not without risk, but they are confident that he has thought it through and will likely be very successful.

Three Who Made the Transition

You may be reading this and find yourself discouraged because you have already invested significant time and money in a profession. You know your heart is not in your job, but you feel trapped. If this describes you, please don't feel alone or give up hope. Most of us are not capable of making a decision early in our life about what we will be happy doing at midlife. Let me give you some encouragement from three friends of mine who faced this feeling with courage and found a way to make changes.

Ted felt family pressure early in his life to pursue dentistry. Being an obedient son, he followed the desires of his family and applied himself in dental school and opened a practice. By this time he had invested years of his life and thousands of dollars, including student loans, to have a successful life in a field that served the real needs of people. There was only one problem --he hated looking into people's mouths every day. The thought of living the rest of his life doing something he had grown to hate depressed him. At the same time, Ted took up investing as a distracting hobby. However, as he gained experience and had some success he found that others were seeking his advice on how to manage money. He found great delight in helping them with their finances. It was all he wanted to do. After some long and encouraging discussions with his wife, Ted gained enough confidence from passing the certified financial planner exam to leave the dental profession. The money at first was not what he could have earned as a dentist, but they have never regretted their decision to my knowledge as he has lived the life he was created to do, rather than what others expected him to do.

Another friend of mine, Tom, found himself in a similar situation. He went to a prestigious school and became a successful attorney working for a big firm in a city. While this profession also helps people and provided a big income, Tom found that he hated every minute of his work. All he could think about was flying airplanes during the day. He had earned a pilot's license as a distraction from his job and found that he loved it. In spite of many complications to start over, Tom quit his job as lawyer and worked his way through some advanced certifications in order to secure a job as a pilot. It was very difficult to change, but he has not had any regrets.

Randy is a friend of mine with a similar story. He went to college and upon graduation began a career as a counselor. However, Randy has a gift in music that includes both writing beautiful music based on Scripture and singing. Randy also had another major asset as he made the decision to focus on his music full time. His wife believed he was called to minister in music and encouraged him to shift focus. Randy went on the road with his wife for five years. During this time they lived very frugally on the modest earnings from Randy's ministry, but they found the peace of Christ as they fulfilled God's purpose in this season of life.

Purpose Statement

As you think about these stories and people you know who have made similar midcourse corrections, I would like to end this chapter by challenging you to focus your understanding of a life calling by developing a purpose statement. You may have several statements that cover a variety of the roles you have in your current situation. For example, I have purpose statements for myself in four areas: as a husband, a father, a bank CEO and as a financial counselor. My financial counselor statement is this: "To help others live intentionally by encouraging them to structure their finances to support their life purpose." This statement of my calling is why I have devoted the time to write this book. The statement doesn't have to be a work of art, but it should help you focus your life around a calling. It can serve as a source of inspiration to you to make the changes in your life that would allow you to be the person you were intended to be in your time on this earth.

If you are unclear on your calling in life, now is the time to give it more thought. I would not discourage you from moving forward with the next chapter while you are working out your purpose in life statement because Chapter 4 may assist you in clearing out some of the fog raised in this chapter. However, it's critical for all of us to grapple with our reason for being. Only with clarity on this issue can we truly develop a financial plan that is in sync with our deepest values and calling.

Summary

Knowing what your life purpose or purposes are will bring immediate order to your financial planning. Many wander through life without much intentionality. Those who don't have a clear direction in life end up either in the mindless accumulation of assets, or failing to develop good financial habits because they lack an overriding passion to save for something meaningful in life. Spending time discerning our life purpose will bring clarity to the financial planning process.

Discussion Questions

1. Can you clearly articulate your life purpose(s) at this season of life? If not, develop a written purpose(s) statement for your life.
2. What did you learn about yourself from answering the life purpose questions in the chapter?
3. Are there spiritual dangers that come from a life without a clearly defined purpose?
4. How are your financial practices currently advancing your life purpose(s)? How are they detracting from you accomplishing your life purpose?
5. Psalm 1 encourages readers to avoid the "counsel of the wicked." What counsel is currently impacting the way you are managing your money? Is it consistent with a purposeful money management philosophy?
6. What is one thing you should change in your current financial practices that would better support your calling from God?

PART II

Your Relationship with Money

CHAPTER 4

Transforming Your Relationship with Money from the Inside Out

"The unexamined life is not worth living."
                                                    Socrates

"...you shall know the truth, and the truth shall set you free."
                                           Jesus (John 8:32)

My uncle Virl was a hard working farmer and a man of few words. However, he had one story that always fascinated me even as a child. He began his farming career just before the depression in the 1930's. Uncle Virl and my Aunt Roellen bet everything they had on becoming farmers. By watching their expenses, managing the land wisely and working long and hard hours, they became very successful. However, they made one critical financial mistake that cost them dearly. As the economy began to turn bad in the 1930's they continued to have positive cash flow, but they put all their profits into the local bank that was close to the farm.

Unfortunately, that bank became a casualty of the depression, and my aunt and uncle lost every penny of their hard earned capital. I was probably five years old when I heard that story for the first time, but the powerful influence it had on shaping my worldview about the fleeting nature of money continues to this day.

Everyone has a number of these core stories buried deep that influence our relationship with money. For example, a second powerful narrative for me came from my parents who instilled the financial rules for going to college. As part of that plan, we were all instructed early in our lives that my parents would pay for a portion of our college, but we were expected to earn enough money to pay for much of it too. As a child I had no idea what it would cost, but I knew it would be a lot. As a result, I can never remember not working in some capacity to earn money growing up. We did a little bit of everything. Mowing lawns and baling hay in the summer. Paper routes all year brought in income. We only had an acre of land, but my dad made sure we made the most of that little acre and had us raising two cows at a time, chickens and strawberries among other business ventures to raise money for that future event of paying for college. Sometime in those early years my parents opened a bank account for me. I'll never forget the fascination of how they would take me to the Savings and Loan with my little blue passbook to see how much interest I had earned on my savings that would help with college expenses. My first exposure to the concept of the magic of compound interest seemed mystical. Through those early years I came away with a deeply ingrained understanding that hard work was rewarded with money that should be saved because it would lead to a better life.

Writing your inner story

What are your earliest memories of money? Have you ever considered how your childhood impressions of how money works might have continued to impact you today? Charles Dickens was perhaps the earliest proponent of the value of revisiting childhood memories as he showed in taking Ebenezer Scrooge back in time in his famous book, *A Christmas Carol*.[xxxii] Part of Scrooge's rehabilitation was revisiting his past because it helped him transform from the stingy Scrooge to the generous man who has captured our imaginations for over 170 years. It is a beautiful picture of how renewal can occur in our relationship with money.

Our beliefs, formed early in life, will guide us blindly into some good and some bad financial decisions unless we take the time to examine them and see both the strengths and weaknesses of our relationship with money. In my case I know that the values I grew up with have been profitable in many ways. For example, I have never had a hard time saving money or working hard in life. Those are generally good attributes. However, I've also noticed that I tend to worry about how I might lose my capital. I can easily think up scary scenarios that show runaway inflation or another depression that could substantially wipe out much of what I have earned. Or, my commitment to savings can lead me to compulsively recalculate my net worth far more often than is necessary to be a good steward of what has been given to me. I've also noticed that for compulsive savers like me, it can become hard to enjoy the blessings God has given if it involves spending some money on ourselves or others. In other words, our strengths can also become our greatest weaknesses in handling money.

A healthy exercise is to think back into your childhood about the most significant memories you have about your experiences with money. After reflecting on those memories, it's helpful to put in writing your inner story on how you are wired to deal with money. This inner story too often has real power to control your finances subconsciously. I'm convinced that the process to having peace with our money includes evaluating the core, perhaps unconscious, beliefs that govern how we interact with money. As we understand ourselves better, only then do we begin to adjust our behavior to the healthier pattern of money management that God intends for us.

We often think in terms of external factors that would make us happy if we could just change them. For example, "If I could just get my student debt paid off I'd be happy." Or, "Once I reach $500,000 in net worth I will be able to relax and enjoy life." But the place to start is not with these, perhaps legitimate goals, but with understanding what is driving our actions internally.

My inner story of hard work, budgeting and saving has a lot of wisdom, but I've come to understand that it's insufficient to find the financial shalom that I think God intended for me to have. As I've transformed my thinking, I've grown to also appreciate the joy in spending money on myself and others as a part of God's plan. I've also grown in my understanding of how easily a big bank account can become the idolatry that Scripture warns us about. Turning what is good--money--into something that is ultimate, brings with it worries and a lack of trusting God's providential control. In short, it's still a learning process for me, but I think it is where the journey to financial shalom should begin.

So before you move on, pause now and reflect on the earliest memories you have about money. Who influenced you? What event(s) that happened in your childhood regarding money is still in your mind? Write them down and try to process whether they are controlling the way you handle money today. Many of us will find that we have held onto a childish view of money because of one or more of these influences. It is only as we become aware of these belief systems governing our behavior that we can begin the change process to a more mature relationship with money.

Finding out how you are wired: the Quiz

In addition to reflection on our inner story, there are other resources to help us understand our relationship with money. These include money personality and money psychology tests. The good news is that many of them are free and very helpful in our effort to renew our thinking according to God's word. As with any assessment tool, the goal is objective self-awareness and, if we are married, to also understand how our spouse processes money decisions in ways that might be different from our own. But as Christians, we can also use these tools to help us focus on where we need to transform our thinking to be more Christ-like in our understanding and use of money.

Most money type quizzes use 4-10 personality categories. My favorite one breaks down our money type into one or more of eight financial archetypes. It was created by Brent Kessel, author of "It's Not About the Money,"[xxxiii] who has given me permission to let you take the quiz at the end of this chapter. If you want to take the online version of this quiz it can be found at abacuswealth.com/quiz. Before reading on, I encourage you to turn now to the end of this chapter and take the short quiz so you can know which of the eight financial archetypes you are.

The Eight Money Types and Scriptures to Renew our Minds

Before diving into each financial archetype, here is a short description of each:
1. The Guardian is always alert and careful.
2. The Pleasure Seeker prioritizes pleasure and enjoyment in the here and now.

3. The Idealist places the greatest value on creativity, compassion, social justice or spiritual growth.
4. The Saver seeks security and abundance by accumulating more financial assets.
5. The Star spends, invests or gives away money to be recognized, feel hip or classy, and increase self-esteem.
6. The Innocent avoids paying significant attention to money, believing that life will work out for the best.
7. The Caretaker gives and lends money to sacrifice themselves for the success of others.
8. The Empire Builder thrives on power and innovation to create something of enduring value.

Here's a more in-depth look at the strengths and weaknesses of each category and where transformation efforts may be needed. As you reflect on your money type, be open to the possibility that you can change your relationship with money as needed.

1. **Guardian**

    Guardians are afraid of something going terribly wrong. They are prone to worry and anxiety. "I might lose my job or business," or "Where are we going to find money if one of us has a medical crisis?" are common fears to keep them up at night. Consequently, they are many times afraid to take risks. They are likely to keep the money they have in very conservative investments like money markets that pay almost nothing and offer no long-term appreciation potential. They may not be a lot of fun to hang around with because they are such hand wringers about potential dangers. However, they have good traits in that they are alert and on the lookout for danger. They will find encouragement in Scriptures like Proverbs 22:3 "A prudent man sees danger and takes refuge, but the simple keep going and suffer for it." They probably have a six month emergency fund as commonly encouraged by financial advisors, have little or no debt, have a will, and may over-insure themselves.

Guardians should meditate on God's call to not worry. Matt 6:25-34 from the Sermon on the Mount is instructive for those struggling with worry. The parable of the talents in Matt 25: 14-30 should also provide encouragement for the positive optimism that should be evident in the believer who trusts God has called him or her to take risks in this life. Proverbs 16:3 contains practical wisdom of encouragement that comes from committing our plans to the Lord and moving forward. The Guardian will benefit from associating with pleasure seekers, idealists and empire builders who can help them balance their money worldview.

Transformed Guardians will resist the urge to fear it can only get worse. They will stop trying to control everything and avoid seeing change as a threat. They will say yes to taking responsibility for what is theirs to do and letting the rest go.

2. The Pleasure Seeker
More than anything else the Pleasure Seeker believes that money is to be used to enjoy life. You might hear them say they aim to die broke or die owing the banks a lot of money they spent on themselves (ouch!). They are sometimes reacting to parents who raised them in a Spartan way. Above all, they purchase for sensory pleasure. They

frequently don't save any of their income, debts may exceed assets and spending on luxury items frequently creates tension in marriage. The ultimate dysfunctional Pleasure Seeker operates under the drug addict mindset, unable to save for tomorrow at the expense of immediate gratification. They find comfort in biblical verses like Eccl 2:24-26 that emphasize enjoyment in eating, drinking and work that comes from the hand of God.

Pleasure Seekers seeking transformation should meditate on Scriptures regarding the dangers of hedonism such as Proverbs 21:17. Jesus' example of denying himself to give us life is the ultimate challenge for the pleasure seeker. Matt 16:24 requires that anyone seeking to be a follower of Jesus to deny himself and is a challenge to the hedonistic worldview. The Christian life is a paradox for the Pleasure Seeker in that we are to count it all joy in the midst of suffering (James 1:2). Savers and Guardians have insights to offer her to offset the dysfunctional behaviors.

Transformed Pleasure Seekers will cease to be addicted to momentary pleasures and say no to using money to mindlessly escape. They will learn to suppress a self-indulgent life that is unhealthy and irresponsible. However, they will still say yes to healthy pleasures and leading a joy filled life, but develop the ability to enjoy spending money on others. They will learn to pause before spending money and start reflecting on the implications. The transformed Pleasure Seeker will find deep and sustained joy as they evolve and focus their gifts and attention on others.

3. **The Idealist**

More than any other money type, Idealists are distrustful of and antagonistic towards money. They may feel like outsiders in business circles or around those with wealth. They are wired to think, "Money is the root of all evil," "I'd be a sellout if I had more money," "Money isn't happiness," "Those with money are corrupt." They may feel guilty if they have money and wring their hands over philosophical questions like, "How can I have so much when others have so little?" Even if it's not conscious, Idealists' aversion to money often leads to an imbalanced and unsatisfying financial life. Idealists are naturally drawn to social activists or spiritual seekers wanting a life without money concerns. If they invest at all, it is likely in nonprofit credit unions, art, or music because they distrust big business. Christians are often Idealists because they are interested in social justice and are full of vision and compassion. They delight in Scriptures that are full of compassion and concern for the poor and oppressed. (Amos 2:7, Luke 4:18) Since those concerns are consistent with a Biblical worldview they reinforce their natural predisposition of the righteousness of their feelings about money being evil.

Idealists should consider that wealth comes from God and is considered a blessing (Deut 8:18, Deut 28:1-14, Mal 3:10-12). God used many wealthy people to achieve his purposes in such as Abraham and Job. Jesus associated with rich and poor. The rich are commanded to use their wealth for redemptive purposes. (I Timothy 6: 17-19, Pr 28:27). In addition, the Ten Commandants establish the basis for private property found in Western civilization in the eighth and tenth commandments. (Don't steal; don't covet your neighbor's property) Idealists would do well to get to know and appreciate Empire Builders who are using their money to change the world for good, or Savers, who accumulate money for specific purpose oriented life goals.

Transformed Idealists will cease feeling guilty over accumulating wealth for godly purposes and say no to trying to soak the rich merely because they have money. They will continue to love all neighbors, rich and poor, by promoting their welfare.

4. **The Saver**

In the Saver's life, money usually represents security, stability, and protection. Savers think their savings are essential to their survival, or negatively equate lack of savings with financial ruin. For these reasons, money takes on god-like importance for Savers, often leading to a frequent desire to count up their savings. I know some users of an online aggregation program called "Mint" that love to see the change in their net worth each day. They give fanatical attention to rate of returns, and create stress with a spouse who is not also a natural saver. They fall into the trap of thinking if they could accumulate "enough" money they would be secure, but enough always increases when the goal is reached. They never spend more than they earn, and don't spoil their children. Some Scriptures encourage the Saver's instincts, especially in passages like Proverbs 6:6-8 that uses the metaphor of the ant storing provisions in summer.

Savers are lionized by the popular money press, but their spiritual pitfalls are real. When we think we are self-sufficient, we can tend to forget God. Jesus cut to the heart of the matter in dealing with the rich young ruler in Mark 10:17-25. Instead of endorsing his self-justifying obedience of a few of the commandments, Jesus tells the man who found his identity in his wealth to go sell all he owned and give it to the poor. The young man quickly finds that Jesus has gone to the heart of his hidden idol of riches. Similar verses for savers to mediate on include Pr. 11:25 and Luke 12:13-21. Savers can benefit by learning to spend money on others and themselves as found in Caretakers and Pleasure Seekers. They can learn to take risks by studying the ways of the Empire Builder and learn to be more hopeful as practiced by the Innocent.

Transformed Savers will stop believing they'll only have what they can possess. They will learn to recognize the folly that clutching money doesn't bring life. They will quit sacrificing joy to a false idol of "getting enough." They will learn to enjoy giving and receiving, feeling safe in God's hands, and possessing true wealth in Christ.

5. **The Star**

Stars are driven by the desire for attention, recognition, significance and respect. This way of life affects most of their financial decisions, including how much to spend and what to spend it on. If they think spending money will buy them the center of attention, they will pay for it. This may lead to a budget heavily weighted towards clothes and prioritizing ways to improve physical attractiveness. Some Stars may use charitable giving to impress people and attract social attention. At their best, Stars can be great leaders or preachers and use their trend setting influence to positively impact the culture.

The Star must guard against pride. Jesus specifically addresses the idea of giving secretly in Matt 6:3-4 as a way to temper one's use of money for showing off our own righteousness. Stars can learn from the Idealist that spiritual growth comes from within and with God's approval being paramount. Combining the Star's visibility with the Idealist's passion for social justice can produce a powerful leadership style. Proverbs 12:9 also tempers the Star's instincts to live above his or her means.

Transformed Stars stop letting others determine their value because of the image they project and will instead find their worth in God. They will learn to quit evaluating themselves only through the eyes of others and to lusting after the approval of others. The Evolved Star will be seeking the approval of God through Jesus' work and be cultivating the inner beauty that comes from being filled with the Spirit of God.

6. The Innocent

The Innocent struggles to master money to the extent necessary to create long term financial stability. Unlike Idealists, Innocents aren't necessarily against money, but they have an ongoing experience of always running short of funds and are generally confused by money. Those who inherit money can't seem to hold onto it. Those who have never had excess money feel like it is an unattainable goal.

Innocents often have credit card debt and don't have an emergency fund; they are in a never ending struggle for survival and are frequent cases for the deacons to work with in churches. They would rather do just about anything than balance the checkbook and often overdraw their checking account simply because they don't know how much money they have. However, Innocents have an innate hope that things will work out. That sense of wonder can be a positive trait that is lost in many of us as our psyches turn rigid in meeting the demands of adulthood.

Innocents sometimes think they have a great relationship with money. They may not believe they need a book like this. I Corinthians 13:11 says that there is a time to put away childish ways and is good meditation material for the Innocent. Proverbs 12:24 states that diligent hands will rule which is what is required in managing finances today. Luke 14:28 tells us that Jesus does not want a blind, naïve commitment that expects only blessings. As a follower of Christ, He expects commitment of those who count the cost. Innocents can learn from Savers who are disciplined in putting money to work for them for established goals and Guardians who are alert to dangers.

Transformed Innocents will stop blaming others for their financial problems. They will no longer be content to be incompetent in handling their money. They will stop feeling sorry for themselves, and will learn about their finances. They can retain their creativity and hopefulness about the future, but gain the freedom that comes from taking responsibility for finances.

7. **The Caretaker**
The Caretaker gives and lends money to express compassion and generosity. They use their time and money to assist their immediate family members, but often extend that help to others too. Some sacrifice themselves financially for others, whether it is necessary or not. They put the needs of others before their own and may develop a god complex of being the savior of others. Sometimes Caretakers don't have a choice in helping, like when a special needs child comes along. They will spend a large portion of their income on others in need. Caretakers keep their investments in low-yielding, but liquid accounts because they are thinking they will have to rescue someone. Scripture supports Caretakers in that Jesus said it "is better to give than to receive." Empathy and generosity are virtues to be commended. The Proverbs 31 woman is an example of a Caretaker that Scripture commends.

The pitfalls of a Caretaker exhibit themselves when it branches into being an enabler of a slothful person. If the self-abandoning results in dependency of the recipient then it is no longer a virtue. The Scriptures have clear teaching on this principle in many places including 2 Thess. 3:10 that teaches a man shouldn't eat if he won't work. Another example is in the Old Testament practice of caring for the poor through gleaning the fields (Deuteronomy 24:19-21.) Proverbs 10: 4-5 is yet another verse for consideration by the enabling Caretaker because it warns about the negligent son that sleeps during harvest. The Caretaker can find balance from the Pleasure Seeker and learn to meet their own needs too. The Empire Builder often gets those in need off of welfare through creation of self sustaining jobs. The Caretaker should study the ways of the Empire Builder to ensure that their helping of those in need does not cause long term dependency and harm of the one they are trying to help.

Transformed Caretakers will stop being a victim of other's needs. They will find their worth in Jesus and not in having to prove their worth through care of others. They will learn to respect themselves and others by making sure their charity is not enabling long term dependency. They will resolve to living with compassion and caring within the guidelines of biblical welfare.

8. The Empire Builder

Most Empire Builders don't necessarily crave a large amount of money or a legacy. They are visionaries who believe that they will be happy when they have made a significant and lasting contribution to the world. This may be in a business or nonprofit environment like a church. Deep inside they believe they will be somebody when they have changed the world in some way. They often do make significant contributions that we enjoy today. If not for Empire Builders almost all the comforts and conveniences of life today would not exist. Empire Builders have a strong work ethic because their identity is tied up in their work. They think about it all the time. They won't pull money out of their business even when it would embrace good financial planning principles to diversify. Their net worth is tied up mostly in their business. They thrive on power or innovation to create something of enduring value. Scripture gives support to the Empire Builder in places like the "dominion mandate" in Gen 1:28 to go out and subdue the earth.

However, they can fall into temptation in areas of greed and stepping on others to achieve their goals. Scriptures that might be helpful to the Christian Empire Builder include Col 3:5 that encourages us to put to death greed which is idolatry. Or Eccl 2:20-23 which causes us to reflect on what happens to the wealth we leave behind. Empire Builders can learn from Caretakers that compassion and generosity are also important financial stewardship principles to practice. Guardians can also provide needed balance to the Empire Builder who is so confident in his own business skills that they fail to see the coming storm clouds and many times go from boom to bust because they keep all their eggs in one basket.

Transformed Empire Builders will learn to put constraints around their pursuit of their vision to avoid stepping on others. They will learn to recognize that God gives wealth for purposes of compassion and generosity and will pursue those goals along with building of the empire. They will learn to balance family and work to avoid making the empire a false idol.

Money and Change (No pun intended)

Let's talk a little about the change process now that you know more about yourself and your relationship with money. I'm convinced that there is real value in working through our internal money issues in the context of a community of friends. This is especially true when we might see that we need to change and could benefit from the accountability that comes from sharing openly with trustworthy friends. As I've used this exercise in the past it has been enlightening and fun to share each participant's archetype with others in the group, and open up the discussion on a deeper level. Married couples in particular have benefited from understanding how their spouse and they differ in their inner core when it comes to money. The good news is that each archetype has something to offer to others. If you and your spouse are opposites, that can be positive if you look at the results as complementary. Take what is good about your strengths and put it to work in your relationship, but also work on the potential downsides together.

Again, remember that Jesus warns us that wealth is deceitful. Therefore, as we approach a close examination of how we deal with money, we need to be on guard against self deception. Romans 1: 18 is particularly interesting in the assertion that we "suppress the truth" about what may be known about God by our wickedness. Verses 29 through 32 list many sins that mankind is guilty of, including two "money" sins: greed and envy. How do we suppress the truth when it comes to money issues? One way is we all know that we ought to be generous, but easily rationalize (suppress?) why we can't be. Or, we know that we should be self-controlled and live within our means, but justify going into credit card debt because of a feeling that we deserve a certain standard of living. The bottom line is that our inner money problems may spring from a spiritual problem that has impacted all of us since the time of Adam's fall in the garden.

As you review the results of the test you took and your earliest memories about money, you should be open to the possibility that you need spiritual transformation in your view of and relationship with money. It's important from a kingdom perspective to recognize that we are all mutually broken in our relationship with God and money, but that each of us also has unique spiritual gifts and financial wiring to contribute to a holistic view of money. This is particularly important in the case of a married couple who may be having conflict over money issues and unable to understand what the other could possibly know about managing money.

Romans 12:2 tells us, "Do not be conformed any longer to the pattern of this world, but be transformed by the renewing of your mind." As we look at the different ways God has wired us to deal with money, it's important to be engaged in actively using the Scriptures to renew our mind into a transformational state that allows us to think differently than the pattern of the world or the pattern we grew up with. Without this renewal, which ultimately springs from a belief that it's Jesus' righteousness at work in our soul giving us the power to change, we remain in bondage to money traps that prevent us from living out lives that are truly free.

Summary

You will probably recognize yourself in two or three of the money archetypes described in this chapter. The goal of this recognition is to first encourage an understanding of our own internal wiring as God has made us and as experience has molded us. As we understand more about why we handle money the way we do, we are not left without hope of ever changing. The Bible speaks to issues of money and wealth extensively and therefore we have great opportunity to see God transform us into more of what He intended for us in our relationship with money. I believe that as God transforms our internal thought life to be more in the image of our Lord that we will find this peace.

Discussion Questions

1. What are three of your earliest memories about money? How have they influenced your relationship with money today?
2. How have your childhood impressions about money been beneficial in how you relate to money? How have they contributed to dysfunctional behavior?
3. Reflect on your relationship with money and write your "inner story." What needs to be transformed?
4. What personality type are you according to the Quiz? In what ways are you naturally wired for success with money? What are the areas you need to work on? Develop one action step that you can take immediately.
5. If you are married, discuss the potential areas for conflict based on your money types. How can you benefit from your spouse's natural money strengths?
6. What Scriptures would be helpful to meditate on to begin transforming your inner thought life about money?

FINDING YOUR FINANCIAL ARCHTYPES

Take the following multiple-choice quiz to confirm your intuitions. More than one answer may apply, in which case, please choose up to three answers that best describe your relationship to money. For the most up-to-date quiz that automatically calculates your financial archetypes, please visit www.abacusweath.com.

QUESTIONS	ARCHETYPES
1. Money *primarily* allows (or would allow) me to:	
☐ Not worry	**Guardian**
☐ Buy things and experiences that I enjoy	**Pleasure Seeker**
☐ Create freedom from other pursuits (i.e. creative, spiritual, political, philanthropic)	**Idealist**
☐ Have an ever-growing sense of security and abundance	**Saver**
☐ Have a sense of importance and recognition from family, friends, and society at large	**Star**
☐ Have faith that things will always work out for the best in the end	**Innocent**
☐ Take care of others, sometimes at my own expense	**Caretaker**
☐ Put time and money into something that makes a lasting impact (e.g., my business)	**Empire Builder**

2. **When it comes to money, at my most extreme, I'm:**

☐	Avoidant and sometimes confused	**Innocent**
☐	Generous, perhaps to the point of being enabling or self-abandoning	**Caretaker**
☐	Impulsive and pleasure-seeking	**Pleasure Seeker**
☐	Frugal and disciplined	**Saver**
☐	Worried and anxious much of the time	**Guardian**
☐	Distrustful or mystified	**Idealist**
☐	Grandiose and ambitious much of the time	**Empire Builder**
☐	Hungry for attention and praise	**Star**

3. **Over the last five years, my financial net worth has:**

☐ Grown, primarily due to good saving and investing habits	**Saver**
☐ Declined, primarily due to lack of focus or gifts to family/friends	**Innocent, Caretaker**
☐ Grown, primarily due to job-related promotions, bonuses, or stock options, or growth in the value of homes), a business, or investment portfolio	**Empire Builder, Star**
☐ Declined, primarily due to overspending	**Pleasure Seeker, Star**
☐ Not kept me from feeling nervous	**Guardian**
☐ I have no idea or don't think it's important	**Innocent, Idealist**

4.	**Which of the following "rules" do you seem to mostly live by?**	
	☐ You can't take it with you, so you might as well enjoy it now.	**Pleasure Seeker, Star, Innocent**
	☐ It is better to give than to receive.	**Caretaker, Idealist**
	☐ A penny saved is a penny earned.	**Saver, Empire Builder**
	☐ Big corporations and/or government can't be trusted.	**Idealist, Empire Builder**
	☐ If I'm not vigilant, it could all fall apart.	**Guardian**
5.	**Which of the following has been most true of me over the past three years?**	
	☐ I have been financially dependent on others (including credit cards or other debts).	**Pleasure Seeker, Idealist, Star, Innocent**
	☐ Others have been financially dependent on me (including employees).	**Caretaker, Saver, Empire Builder**
	☐ There are no dependencies either way.	**Guardian, Saver**

6. **What I have to show (financially) is:**	
☐ A lot of "stuff" that I've bought over the years	**Pleasure Seeker**
☐ I don't have investments (other than possibly a home)	**Innocent**
☐ Ownership in a closely held business or real estate	**Empire Builder**
☐ Financial investments like stocks, income property, or mutual funds	**Saver**
☐ Socially screened stocks, collectibles, or my creative or academic work	**Idealist**
☐ A showpiece home, nice cars, a restaurant or retail business, wine, jewelry, or art	**Star**
☐ Parents, adult children, charities, or friends who wouldn't have made it without my help	**Caretaker**
☐ Mostly fixed income investments such as bank savings accounts, CDs, bonds, or T-bills	**Guardian**

Now, for each box that you checked above, place a tally mark next to the archetype name(s) that correspond to your answer. For example, if for question 4 you selected the first answer, you should put a tally mark next to Pleasure Seeker, Star, and Innocent. If you selected the last answer, you should only put a tally mark next to Guardian.

Transforming Your Relationship with Money from the Inside Out

_____ Guardian   _____ Pleasure Seeker

_____ Idealist   _____ Saver

_____ Innocent   _____ Star

_____ Empire Builder   _____ Caretaker

Now add up your tally marks for each archetype, and list the top three in order from the most dominant to the least:

_____

_____

_____

CHAPTER 5

Raising Your Money Consciousness to Live the Abundant Life

"Money is a good servant, but a bad master."
                                    Charles Spurgeon

"Watch out! Be on your guard against all kinds of greed; a man's life does not consist in the abundance of his possessions."
                                    Jesus, Luke 12:15

Jim and Angi are two of my former customers. Together they earn an income well over $200,000 yet they came into my bank with a predicament. They had been unable to live on "only" $200,000 and had racked up credit card debt of over $150,000 along with their mortgage, car loans and student debt. After evaluating their finances, we were able to restructure their debt by taking a second mortgage on their house and some other collateral to pay off the high interest credit card debt. For the moment their cash flow was above water and, if they followed the plan, they would be able to dig out from under this mountain of debt. Unfortunately, Jim and Angi had not really learned their lesson, and in less than two years they came back into the bank having barely made a dent in repaying the $150,000, but also having racked up an additional $200,000 in new credit card debt. Clearly, no matter how much this couple might be able to earn in their professional jobs, their spending would outstrip the inflow unless there was a change in their relationship with money. Rather than money serving them, it had become their master.

The goal of this chapter is to examine ways to improve the way we interact with money to make it our servant, rather than our master. We want to not only avoid a situation like the one Jim and Angi were faced with, but also increase our money consciousness to make sure our money decisions are supporting our life purpose. We'll look at five steps that hold the potential to radically change your money decision making process to support a more intentional and purposeful life.

Step One: Track your net worth

A fundamental tenet of a Christian view of money is that we don't actually own it, it belongs to God. We are stewards, or trustees, of his money. If that's the case, the first step in fulfilling duties of a trustee is to have a reliable accounting of what the assets are. So, if we adhere to the Biblical principle of stewardship, we must regularly take stock of the assets and personal net worth we have been given to oversee for our Creator.

But there are other reasons to at least annually calculate your personal net worth. My wife and I have spent time every year since 1986 going over our financial statement. In addition to contributing to good communication in our marriage, this practice has also been an incredible opportunity for reflection on God's goodness and blessing to our family. We've seen our net worth go up and down from year to year, but with almost 30 years of data to look back on, it is amazing now to remember the lean years and to give thanks to God for the blessings of wealth He has bestowed on our family.

Many of us dream of a life free of money worries. We have a passion we would like to pursue if we were only freed from the need to earn a paycheck. A net worth calculation can serve as a general guideline of how close we are to that financial goal. Let me explain. Many financial planners use a 4% rule for calculating how much of your net worth can be withdrawn without running out of money over a 30 year retirement period. William Bengen, a financial planner, first published an article in 1994 that showed how a 4% withdrawal rate, increased every year for inflation, should have a 90% chance of not running out of money for a normal retirement if the financial assets are invested in a mix of stocks and bonds.[xxxiv] For two decades this rule of thumb has been widely used by other planners, although some have begun to suggest lowering the 4% somewhat to account for a low interest rate environment. For example, if we have $500,000 of investable assets (not including our home), we should under normal circumstances be able to withdraw 4%, or $20,000, a year for a 30 year time period without running out of money if we have a proper asset mix. Theoretically, you should be able to increase this amount by the rate of inflation each year. If you know, for example, that your current living expenses are $30,000 a year, you can easily see that you either need to reduce your living costs by $10,000 a year, or increase your financial assets to $750,000 before you can quit your day job. If you have a job that also pays a pension or if you qualify for social security, you could add that payout to the 4% total to see if it is sufficient to cover your living expenses without your paycheck. So, if you receive social security of $5,000 a year, the amount you need in invested funds is reduced to $625,000. While this 4% test is an excellent rule of thumb, sudden market gyrations may happen that will require periodic reevaluations.

I have seen this tool help connect some dots about money for even the most innocent money managers. For example, I once worked with a 20-something young lady who really didn't care about money, or need much to live on, but she still had to do some fundraising for her ministry. As I talked to her about the advantages of a Roth IRA, it dawned on her that if she put away a modest amount each year she could one day be free to do ministry without having to raise money. Suddenly the light bulb came on and she has been diligently investing her modest funds in pursuing this goal ever since.

Make it a habit to calculate your net worth at least once a year, and use that opportunity to reevaluate your purpose and calling and compare it to your financial resources. As we discussed in Chapter 3, work is good and should be aligned with our life calling, so our goal is not necessarily to gather enough wealth to quit working. However, many individuals find the passion they once had for a job begins to wane as they grow older, but an offsetting desire begins to grow in them to pursue work that may pay very little or nothing. Once we begin developing an awareness of our purpose in life, and the ways that focus may be changing, the net worth calculation can serve as a motivator to spend less and earn more to achieve the financial means to fund our next calling.

Unless you have a complicated financial situation, the development of a statement of net worth should be fairly easy. If you have a more complicated financial structure, your friendly community banker or accountant should be very happy to assist you in this effort. However, here is a simple version of a net worth statement that should suffice for most readers. This is the actual statement for my wife and me in 1986:

Financial Statement
As of 12-31-1986

Assets		**Liabilities**	
Liquid Assets:			
Checking account	$1,200	Credit card debt	$0
Money Market fund	4,300	Car loans	$0
Total Liquid Assets	$5,500	Student loans	$0
Invested Assets:		Mortgage	$44,000
20th Century mutual	$1,550	Total debt	$44,000
Prospector fund	650		
GNMA fund	100	Net Worth	$39,500
IRA	2,700	Total Debt and NW	$83,500
Bank stock	8,000		
Church bond	1,500		
Total Invested assets	$14,500		
Fixed Assets:			
Cars	$8,500		
Residence	55,000		
Total Fixed Assets	$63,500		
Total Assets	$83,500		

You can create your own balance sheet and compute your net worth by simply plugging in your assets and liabilities into these categories:

Liquid Assets: List any assets that you have immediate access to such as: Checking accounts, savings accounts, money market funds, E-bonds or I-bonds, cash buried under your mattress, or cash in your wallet.

Invested assets: List any assets that are in stocks, bonds, mutual funds, gold or other hard assets that a market can be found to sell them in, cash surrender value life insurance, retirement accounts all would be examples of assets in this section.

Fixed assets: List any real estate including your personal residence, cars, your estimate of the value of your business, if you own one, in this section.

Debt: List principle balances on your credit cards, car loans, mortgages or any other debt you owe.

Net Worth: Add all your assets up and then subtract all of your debt to estimate your net worth.

To calculate how close you are to financial independence using the 4% rule, you would exclude any fixed assets such as your house or car. In my example, my wife and I had $20,000 of investable assets. Taking this number times 4%; we would have had only $800 a year to live off of if I had decided to retire in 1986. With five children, I was not in a position to quit just yet! You will want to compare your number to your current expenses, which we will discuss in step 3, to determine how much of a gap exists in your ability to live on only your investments, without a paycheck.

You should perform this calculation once a year and reflect on how it has changed from the year before. Are you going forward or backward? Do you need to change the way you are investing or spending your resources based on the results? How close are you to achieving a nest egg sufficient to fund moving forward with your dream? All of these questions and more are ways to raise your money consciousness and help provide the motivation to make appropriate changes either on the income or expense side of your income statement.

Step 2: Awareness of Money Flow into Your Life

Most of us are so day to day oriented that we lose perspective on how much money has flowed through our fingers. So, I have found a benefit from the following exercise, which can cause us to pause and reflect on where it all went! And this, of course, builds our resolve to make changes. Any American that has paid into the social security system can go to SSA.gov and get a printout of the lifetime earned income. Having been in the workforce for 40 years, it is really an eye opening experience for me.

For younger workers however, it is not that difficult to calculate the potential lifetime money flow that is within your reach. For example, if you are currently making the US median average of $50,000, merely multiplying that times 40 years would get a non-inflation adjusted total of $2,000,000. In other words, even an average earner in America has a multi-million dollar potential. And, this does not include non- wage money such as gifts or inheritance.

The point of this exercise is to show how powerful you are in bringing in money into your life and to meditate on the implications. We are all prone to self-delusion, but this exercise can focus our minds on what we are capable of achieving in money flow. It should instill confidence in our goal-setting as we begin to focus on actually taking steps to fulfill our calling. For some this exercise can be an angry wakeup call when we realize how much money has come in if we have little to show for it. That anger can be a good thing if we use it as motivation to make changes in our money habits.

Step 3: Awareness of Money Flow out of Your Life

When I do financial counseling, one of the first things I ask is, "Do you know exactly where all your money is going?" Usually there is a lot of nervousness at the question, embarrassment of not having a handle on why the money runs out when making a good salary, and a general feeling that tracking how money is being spent is not all that important to solving the money problems that brought them to me for advice. The reality is that when we only estimate how our money is being spent, we give ourselves way too much credit for being frugal and wise consumers. But even more detrimental is that carelessness in this area leads to a life that is far from intentional.

The first assignment in this step is to track every penny that you spend for three months. This is not an exercise intended to make you squirm. Rather, it is meant to make you conscious of what you are doing when you spend money and to allow you to evaluate the value of every purchase you make against your life goals. Just the process of keeping track of every penny of your spending for a time has been shown to reduce overall spending by a sizeable amount in many cases. However, that is not the goal just yet. What we want to do is to have accurate numbers that reflect how you are spending money. You can create your own categories, but my wife and I generally use these: donations, housing, transportation, food, school/kids, medical, entertainment/vacations, clothes, insurance, investments, debt payments and miscellaneous.

So make a commitment to track every penny for this time period. If you've never done this exercise before, you will be surprised how much more aware of your spending you will become. But it is also critical for the next step when we evaluate your spending in light of what is important to you in achieving your goals in life. To facilitate true internal change in your relationship with money you have to achieve this higher state of awareness.

At the end of the first month, organize the receipts or data that you collected into the categories you have chosen. Spend a little time meditating on what the results tell you about yourself. What surprises you? What doesn't surprise you? Where do you think you are overspending on things that don't bring you joy or support your purpose in life?

Married couples who have never developed good communication around money issues should be prepared for some discomfort at this point in the process. However, I can assure you that once the communication lines are opened through this step, the result can be a more unified marriage.

Step 4: Connecting Purpose to Daily Purchases

What is money? Economists have a variety of definitions including, "a store of value," or "a medium of exchange." However, for our purposes, we need a definition that is far more practical and meaningful. We need a definition so practical that we will be able to connect our daily decisions to buy or not buy a pair of shoes or a latte to our life purpose. Joe Dominguez and Vicki Robin wrote a book called *Your Money or Your Life*[xxxv] that defined money in an incredibly useful way for our purposes. They said, "Money is something we give our life energy for."

How is this definition useful to us in managing our money? Let me show you by starting with a conversion of our life into hours of time available. No one knows how long they will live of course, but for planning purposes we can make assumptions of how much time we have to fulfill our life purpose. You can get your actuarially estimated life expectancy from the Social Security website. This exercise alone is sobering as we consider how little time we have on this earth. If I plug in my age of 58, I see that I am expected to live another 25 years to age 83. Converting this information to hours I get the following table:

Total hours in an 83 year life	727,080
Hours expended in 58 years	508,080
Estimated hours remaining	219,000

The next step in this process is to estimate the hourly price I am selling my life energy to my employer. In other words, how much am I paid for one hour of my limited time on this earth? In order to do this accurately, however, we need to deviate a bit from the way an employer would calculate this number. A wage and hour auditor would say if you are paid $20.00 an hour, then that is what you are trading an hour of your life energy for. However, this ignores too many important factors in this new way of looking at money. First, it fails to take into account the total hours you must put in to do your job. For example, it ignores commuting time, time you spend getting dressed and groomed for work and thinking about work when you are not in the office. It also fails to subtract out of the equation expenses you incur to perform your job such as the cost of commuting, clothes, meals, entertainment costs you incur to de-stress from your work day, expenses you pay for things you could do yourself if you were at home such as lawn care or painting. Each job is unique, but these are some of the hidden costs to perform our daily labor.

Using some of these extra expenses and time traps, you can get a more accurate estimate of how much you are being paid for an hour of your life energy. Here is an example of how you might do this calculation for your own situation assuming a take home salary of $30,000 with some of the costs that I described in the above paragraph:

Estimate of true hourly wage

Take home salary	$30,000
Value of benefits	6,000
Total income	$36,000

Less costs of job

Clothes	$ 500
Commute	3,750
Meals	1,250
Entertainment	1,000
Hired do-it-yourself jobs	1,500
Decompression costs	1,000
Total costs	$9,000
Adjusted Income	$27,000

True hours worked

Hours at job	2,000
Hours commuting	250
Thinking at home	250
Total hours doing work	2500

<u>True pay for an hour of time:</u> $27,000/2,500 = $10.80

So you can see that the difference in what you are told by your boss you are making per hour can be quite different than what you are actually selling your life energy for when all factors are considered. In this case, the stated wage at $30,000 a year would equate to $14.42 for a 40 hour work week. The actual wage of $10.80 is $3.62 (or 25%) less.

But this is not the end of the story. This is just a starting tool that can transform your daily encounters with money decisions. Knowing how much you are selling your life energy for gives you a powerful method to consciously evaluate not just if you are getting paid enough at work, but also to judge every purchase you make for the rest of your life. You will be able to easily consider whether a purchase is worthy of its cost in terms of your life energy and if it is consistent with your life purpose. We'll talk about budgeting in the next chapter, but this is better than budgeting as you can now evaluate your spending in real time in light of what your life energy is worth.

How does this simple calculation give us such a powerful tool? Let me illustrate. Let's assume you are at the mall and thinking about buying a new pair of shoes that are priced at $150.00. In the past, you might have thought about how you could put them on a credit card and pay them off over the next few months along with your other credit card balances. Now however, if you know that you are selling your life energy for $10.80 at work, you can ask yourself a new question: "Are these shoes worth 13.88 hours of my life energy?" In fact, you can now begin to evaluate every purchase you consider in light of this new way of looking at the value of your life energy. Many have used this tool to live more frugal lives, but with higher enjoyment, as they find they only spend money on items that truly bring fulfillment into their lives. My wife and I have used this method for many years and find ourselves joking at times about whether a purchase is worth so much of our life energy. However, it really isn't a joke to be able to better align our spending with what truly matters in our lives.

Here's a framework that I recommend as you evaluate your spending results that you discovered in step two. List all of your purchases for the last month and ask yourself two questions: "Did this purchase support my life purpose?" and "Was this purchase worth the life energy I expended to buy it?" The optimal purchases are those that are both a part of your life purpose and valued to you as worth the life energy spent. However, some purchases, like the chance to meet an old football star and get his autograph, might be worth the expenditure due to the "delight" factor apart from the pure purpose test. You chart might look something like this:

Purchase Item	Cost in $'s	Cost in Life energy?	Part of life purpose?	Worth Life energy Spent?	Final Decision
New shoes	$150.00	13.89 hours	No	No	No
Starbucks with friend	$5.00	0.46 hours	Yes	Yes	Yes
New Car	$30,000	2,777.78 hours	No	No	No
Dick Butkus autograph	$300	27.78 hours	No	Yes	Yes
Harvard Education	$220,000	20370.37 hours	yes	No	No

You should evaluate every purchase in this manner. If you are married, it should lead to some very engaging conversations with your spouse. However, after the first run through of all your expenses, this tool should be a wonderful way for you to lead a more intentional and authentic life as your align your daily spending with your life purpose.

A variation of this tool can also be useful in evaluating the true cost of having both spouses work. For example, if one spouse makes a significant amount of money in a profession and the other spouse makes significantly less per hour, then the calculations they should do would be to compare the income coming in from the lower paid spouse, versus the advantages of being able to have one spouse available for such responsibilities as child care, cooking, cleaning, yard work and generally leading a less hurried life. Many couples with children are actually better off if one spouse does not work because of the resulting savings from the ability to do it yourself, as well as a more peaceful home.

Step 5: Gaining Momentum with Small Wins

Everyone begins a purposeful money system from a different starting point, but it's important psychologically to be able to see progress in your efforts immediately. Here are four suggestions that I have seen others implement that should work for you no matter where you begin the process of raising your money consciousness.

Try a fiscal fast. If you're like me, you've probably tried fasting from food sometime in your life. Whether for weight loss or spiritual enlightenment, one thing I know is that my food consciousness goes up tenfold whenever I practice this discipline. I remember ending my first fast by eating an orange. That orange was probably an average orange, but as I ate it I had a new appreciation for how delicious the taste and smell of a simple orange could be. A gourmet meal prepared by the best chef in the world wouldn't have tasted any better than that orange because I was suddenly aware of joy in eating that I missed when food is taken for granted.

I first became aware of the concept of fiscal fasting in an entertaining book on thrift called, "The Ultimate Cheapskate," by Jeff

Yeager.[xxxvi] In this book the author suggests that you start to break a spending addiction by engaging in spending detox. He suggests going for a week or more each year without spending any money and without stockpiling in advance. It's a fascinating exercise that will immediately heighten your appreciation for how you spend --and waste-- money. I don't necessarily recommend a full week as a required way to start this discipline. For some of us just going a full day without money flowing out of our lives will be a good start. But whatever the time you select, you will find commensurate benefits including rediscovering all the wonderful things that you can do in life that are not connected to money. And don't rush out when it is over and spend what you saved either. Put it to use in paying down some debt or adding to your savings.

Find an accountability partner. While some people exhibit self discipline, most of us do better when we have someone to hold us accountable. Find someone who you respect when it comes to money matters and ask him or her to check in on your progress in implementing the steps laid out in this chapter. While humbling, I believe it is a key step in the direction of giving you a successful relationship with money.

Focus on achieving one goal in three months or less. Many people I have counseled with do not have any savings, and a large percentage of families live paycheck to paycheck with no backup plan. Therefore, I always recommend in such cases that the first goal should be the accumulation of $1,000 in a savings plan. While there may be other possible uses such as paying down high interest credit card debt, I believe that the emotional security that can come from quickly achieving a small goal far outweighs the logical approach that might suggest paying off debt. Or, if you already have a healthy emergency fund, your first goal may be to begin contributing to a 401k program at your work, especially if you are currently not receiving the full employer match. In some ways it doesn't matter exactly what your first goal is as long as it is achievable in three months or less and will be valued by you when it is completed. Discussing your first goal with your accountability partner would also be a good move prior to setting it so you can rejoice together when it is achieved.

Calculate and track your financial independence progress. As you begin to track your expenses each month, graph them on a chart as shown below. Over time, you will likely see a steady decreasing line as you learn to live more fully and frugally. At the same time, begin to track the investable assets that you figured in step 1 at the beginning of this chapter. Multiply your investable assets times 4% divided by 12 and post this number on the same chart. As you begin to grow your investable assets you will see the line graph grow gradually from month to month that represents your income available to live off of from your investable assets. At some point the expense line and the 4% income line will intersect. At that point you will be getting close to having your finances structured in such a way that you could theoretically live indefinitely off of your accumulated capital. The visual representation of this trend will encourage you in at least two ways. First, you will be focused on driving your expenses lower and lower. Second, you will begin to see how you could have financial freedom to live a life free of the hours spent earning a daily paycheck if that is what you are called to do. At a minimum, you will be in touch with your financial position in a new enlightened manner.

Financial Independence Graph

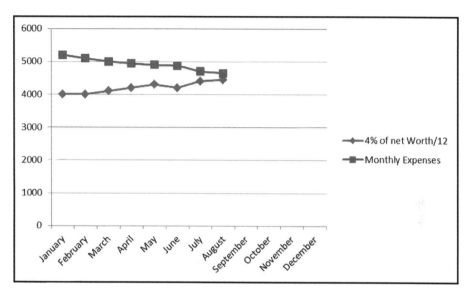

Summary

Raising your money consciousness is critical to living a holistic life with your money integrated into your life purpose. These five steps will put you on the path to living a more intentional life with fewer monetary roadblocks to achieving your goals. All of the steps from this chapter will provide the foundation for the big budget choices we will discuss in Chapter 6.

Discussion Questions

1. How would you rank on a scale of 1 to 10 your own money consciousness? How could improving your money consciousness contribute to a more intentional life?
2. Calculate your net worth. Do you see your net worth as what God has entrusted you to manage? How does a stewardship mentality change your relationship with wealth?
3. How much money do you estimate will flow into your life if you live to an average age? What are your duties for managing that cash flow? What would your grade be up to this point for managing your cash flow?
4. Try connecting your money spending to your life energy. How might this change your spending habits?
5. Where are you on the financial independence graph? Is it a legitimate goal for you to achieve earnings on your invested assets greater than your expenses? Why or why not?

CHAPTER 6

Children and Houses and Cars, Oh My! Managing Money Successfully in Marriage

It's clearly a budget. It's got a lot of numbers in it.
George W. Bush

Suppose one of you wants to build a tower. Will he not first sit down and estimate the cost to see if he has enough money to complete it? For if he lays the foundation and is not able to finish it, everyone who sees it will ridicule him, saying, `This fellow began to build and was not able to finish.'
Luke 14:28-30

I remember watching a TV show a number of years ago and seeing a memorable scene. The husband and wife were arguing over whether or not they could afford a new big screen TV. The father insisted that they could afford it and the mother was more cautious about the purchase. Finally, the father put his foot down and said, "Honey, we can't afford to be pinching pennies when it comes to buying the machine that is going to raise our children!" Managing money in a marriage clearly deserves some special attention.

It Starts with Communication

Ed and Marilyn were referred to me by my pastor. They were planning on getting married soon and Marilyn didn't have a clue about money. However, the good news was that she wanted their marriage to have a firm foundation in this important area. Ed knew some things about money, and actually had put away a significant rainy day fund, but he wasn't certain what the money rules should be in marriage. In my experience, they represent the majority of young couples today who enter marriage not quite sure how much of their independence they should be giving up when it comes to money. It was a privilege to work with such a wonderful young couple who have now been married for quite some time. When I last checked in with them they had put in place a regular system of communication on money matters that has kept them unified and at peace with each other on their path to achieving their financial goals.

Sam and Elizabeth on the other hand came to see me after being married for many years. They had many of the typical problems in married couple's finances: unpaid student loan debt, high interest credit card debt and struggles to keep their bills current every month. Money tensions were sucking all the joy out of their lives. I found there was almost no communication going on between the two of them about their finances. It was awkward, but I pointed out the need for them to start a system of regular communication on their finances. They needed a way to find unity on what their goals should be. I suggested it was critical for them to

Children and Houses and Cars, Oh My! Managing Money Successfully in Marriage

start short monthly meetings to gain agreement on a recurring 30 day plan for how their money would be managed. Several months after starting to implement some regular family meetings they were able to gain control of their finances and begin moving toward building wealth that supported their life purposes.

I mention these two stories because they illustrate the challenges couples face in managing money in the family. It's hard enough to keep finances simple and focused as an individual, but exponentially more challenging when merging two people with differing perspectives and values. However, I know achieving marital harmony in managing money is not only possible, it's actually synergistic when two people come together with agreed upon goals, encourage one another in the process and then celebrate as benchmarks are met. The foundation to this system working is recognizing that when two people come together in marriage, there are no longer two sets of books to manage. The biblical concept of becoming one in marriage includes unity in ownership of assets and debts. If a new marriage is consummated and the husband continues to think of the other spouse's debt as "her debt," then there is not going to be the unity God intends. Or if the wife continues to think of her IRA as "her assets," then she has not fully embraced the concept of oneness in marriage. The exceptions to this principle include when the marriage is a second marriage and there are significant assets and children from the first marriage. The complexity of those situations is beyond the scope of this book because they require a great deal of wisdom dealing with inheritance matters, but in general, the more committed the couple is to merging their finances into joint ownership, the more likely the outcome will be harmonious.

My wife Nancy and I use a simple process each month to keep our communication open and our goals aligned. We keep track of our expenses closely and at the end of the month we add them up and put them into expense categories that we have agreed upon. We then compare the results to what we had agreed would be our spending plan at the beginning of the month. We talk about the differences, but keep it lighthearted. The session usually lasts only five or ten minutes for the review. However, when we talk through the next 30 day plan it can be as short as a few minutes or it can go much longer if we need to talk through a major need in the household or if we are aware of a major charitable cause that could use a helping hand. The point is that we have a workable process in place that gives us a regular venue to review together the money flow that has occurred in our family. We've been at it so long we are quite confident in our partner's judgment on money matters and we rarely have disagreements. We are completely honest about how we spend our money and don't hide any expenditure from each other. It's now a process that works quite smoothly for us and that both of us enjoy. However, for newly married couples, or couples who have been together for years but never talked about money matters, a system like this might be like a Copernican revolution that could be painful at first.

I'll go through some specific techniques you might consider using to open up your spending plan communication at the end of this chapter. But for now, I want to emphasize that if you want to find renewal in your marriage in the area of finances, the underlying requirement is honesty and openness to changing after listening to your partner. It's all about working together and mutually agreeing on your spending priorities in life. The goal should be that all of the discussions about money will be in the context of a bigger life plan that both agree on as the larger purpose God has called you to in your marriage.

Some financial books emphasize controlling the small expenditures to achieve financial success. While I believe it might be

Children and Houses and Cars, Oh My! Managing Money Successfully in Marriage

useful to cut out a latte or two each week if the cost of them do not justify the life energy expended to buy them, I think it's much more important to start with the really big decisions in life first: having children, the size of your house, where you live, and automobiles. These factors usually dominate most of your budget and deserve special attention. Then we'll get to those lattes.

The Big Items in Life

Children – There is perhaps no bigger family economic decision in life, with both dramatic short term and long term implications, than whether to have children--and how many. It is not a theoretical question for me as a father of five! The year 2012 was a particularly interesting year for us with two weddings, two children in college, one child in a private high school, a torn ACL surgery and a new dog. No expense category came close that year to our "children expense" category. To state the obvious, unity is critical on this topic.

Various calculators are available for anyone wanting to estimate the cost of raising children. I found the estimates can be very wide ranging anywhere from approximately $200,000 to $500,000 for one child assuming four years of college expenses at a public university. Of course, these are just estimates and frugal living can dramatically lower one family's total costs compared to a less disciplined one. Nevertheless, having children will clearly be a significant long term expense that many people want to avoid strictly because they are unwilling to pay the price.

So why would anyone want to absorb this multi-year expense of having children? I think for the Christian couple there are many biblical reasons to justify the cost of having children, as well as significant economic and societal reasons for everyone to consider a positive attitude towards procreation.

First and foremost, children are a gift from the Lord. (Ps 127) This view may be at odds with many who see them as expensive and requiring many years of high maintenance time commitments. However, God's ways are not always our ways, and seeing children as a blessing and not a financial curse is the first faithful step to obeying God's creation mandate by multiplying. In the first chapter of Genesis, God addresses this issue when he tells Adam and Eve to "Be fruitful and multiply, fill the earth and subdue it." Gen 1:28. This commandment was issued before sin was introduced into the world. In addition, perhaps to make sure we didn't miss it the first time, God repeated this commandment after the flood. (Gen 9:7) So the command still remains a mandate from our Creator to procreate and fill his world. Jesus gives us a way of life that excludes worrying about the future expenses those children may bring when he taught us to pray: "give us this day our daily bread," not "give us in advance a bank account to pay for our child's expenses." I learned this lesson many years ago when Nancy noticed that I constantly put off having children in order to just save "a little more." At some point, however, with her encouragement, I learned that we were never going to have "enough" to satisfy every possible "what if" contingency. I learned that this is one area of life that is not subject to the normal rules of personal financial planning. Kids are a higher priority, in my opinion, than a perfect financial plan.

Economists are also beginning to recognize the economic disaster that low fertility rates are causing. I can still remember being asked to read "The Population Bomb"[xxxvii] when I was a high school student in the early 70's which warned of mass starvation of humans in the 70's and 80's due to overpopulation. While those hysterical predictions turned out to be completely wrong, they did contribute to the current fertility decline by providing a moral argument for not having children. Now, however, a large number of thoughtful voices are raising alarm bells about disasters that await countries that pursue negative population growth. A book published in 2013 called, *What to Expect When No One's Expecting*, has the thesis that the root cause of most of our (economic) problems is our declining fertility rate. While the replacement rate just to stay even is 2.1 children per woman over the course of her life, we are currently at 1.93.[xxxviii] This book and others point out that growing populations lead to innovation and conservation. This is demonstrated in falling commodity prices and a cleaner environment than existed in the 70's even though the US population has increased by more than 50% since then.[xxxix] However, low fertility countries fail to innovate because, in an aging society, incentives for consumption go toward health care to preserve and extend life. The declining fertility rate is beginning to impact the United States. For example, in 1970 there were 22.2 Americans over age 65 for every 100 who were working. By 2010 those numbers increased to 24.6 and are projected to climb above 40 by 2030 according to US census bureau projections.[xl] This aging of our country will likely put a tremendous strain on our resources and take away from our investment in innovation. So even in a macro economic analysis, God's procreation mandate brings prosperity to the nations that practice it.

But beyond all these religious and economic reasons to be a baby producing family, I believe kids are worth the investment because of the richness of a family life that is full of children and eventually grandchildren. Of course my wife and I could have had a lot more money if we'd never had kids, but the vacuum left from all the rich experiences we've enjoyed could never be filled by more stuff or a bigger bank account.

We should always count the cost of what we do in life before plunging into a project, but having children is different from any other financial decision. It is a decision that is made in faith knowing that God has promised to meet our needs even if the plan is not crystal clear. If I had looked at the cost of having five children over a twenty some year period, I never would have been able to say yes to our decision. In fact, of all spending decisions, I think this is one that you may never be fully ready for mentally or financially. However, speaking for Nancy and me, God has always provided for our needs as He promised. And now that our financial life is stronger, we are able to appreciate the joy of having adult relationships with our children without the constant money drain. Your marriage is unique and these are very personal decisions. However, I hope this provides some thoughtful material to consider as an alternative voice to much of the counsel being given on family and financial planning.

Where to live and how much house? – The biggest purchase most of us will ever make will be a house. Many who want to advise you on what you should buy have a conflict of interest that you should consider before making a decision. The bigger the loan, the more money the bank financing the house makes. The higher the sale price, the more commission the real estate agent will take home. The bigger the new house you build, the more the construction industry makes. I could go on, but my point is that most of us may only buy two or three houses in our lifetime, so we are at an extreme disadvantage when it comes to sorting out what makes the most sense for our situation with so much "free" advice offered by those around us with a vested interest. But whatever housing decision we make will dramatically impact the flexibility of the rest of our budget. Therefore it makes sense to make sure we think through the housing decision carefully to ensure that our house is a blessing and not a curse.

First, how long do you expect to stay in the house? If you are only planning on living in the house for less than five years, you are probably better off renting. The upfront costs of buying a house are significant, and it is likely that unless you stay for five or more years you are better off renting.

Second, how much house should you purchase? One old rule of thumb in the banking industry for the maximum amount you should pay toward expenses including the mortgage, taxes and insurance is 28% of your gross monthly income.[xli] If you make $5,000 a month your monthly mortgage expenses should not exceed $1,400 by this rule of thumb. However, keep in mind that there will be other expenses associated with home ownership including anywhere from 1% to 4% of the cost of the house in annual maintenance and repair bills. When buying a $300,000 home you could expect to add another $500 a month to your cost of home ownership if you averaged 2% of the value of the home in repairs. In other words, if you spend 28% of your gross income on a mortgage, taxes and insurance and another $500 a month on repairs and maintenance, you would now be spending $1,900 on housing a month, absorbing 38% of your gross income not including utilities. And, if you were to reduce your gross income by a conservative 10% to account for social security taxes (7.51%) and federal and state income taxes (2.49%), your housing expense as a percent of net income would rise to over 42% of your take home pay. That doesn't leave much room for donations, food, transportation, and childcare expenses to say nothing of saving for retirement or taking a vacation.

And you really have a tight budget if you incur this suggested level of housing expense and have other debts like student loans or a car payment to make. Another conservative banking industry rule of thumb is that your total debt payments should not exceed 36% of your gross income.[xlii] (Some banks allow much higher levels.) So if you also have a car loan payment of $400 a month, your total housing and debt payments would absorb over 51 percent of your take home pay. If you didn't have a 20% down payment you will also likely end up paying private mortgage insurance for many years. This insurance can vary from around 0.3 percent to 1.15 percent of the original loan amount per year.[xliii] You can see how quickly the excitement of a wonderful new house can turn into a nightmare of financial pressure even when following suggested guidelines. In short, it's possible to end up with a beautiful house, but no life to go along with it because the total debt obligations hamstring the rest of your finances.

But this analysis does not mean that a house cannot be a wonderful investment. Quite the contrary. Congress has given home ownership tax advantages over renting and the prospect of having our house appreciate in value is possible, though not inevitable. The point of this exercise is to make sure that we have run through our own numbers in projecting a budget before purchasing a home. We never want to rely on what our real estate agent tells us we can afford. I can guarantee you that the real estate agent will not be there to help you balance your budget after the sale. Both husband and wife should realistically agree on what they can afford before "falling in love" with a piece of real estate. Use a trusted financial counselor to bounce your plans off of as a check on the validity of your assumptions, and you can have even more confidence in your decision.

Because the housing decision locks so much of your budget down for years to come, it's very important that you not over buy. Get some perspective on how much house you really do need. The sustainability movement has begun to show that we really don't need a lot of square footage to lead meaningful lives. In fact, it's starting to look like its back to the future. The average home size in the 1950's was less than 1,000 square feet. That number steadily grew up to 2300 square feet in the 2000's despite declining household sizes. Now, house sizes are declining, with the median size of a new home in 2010 estimated at 2,169 square feet.[xliv] My point is not to argue over the virtues of a small house, it is merely to say that the size of a house has little bearing on the quality of life of the family living in it. The quality of life can and does go down in a large house that creates excessive pressure on the budget.

Where to live is an equally important question that has huge financial consequences. Many older individuals who have worked in high cost locations have done the math and realized that they can quit jobs they no longer have a passion for if they are willing to move to a lower cost location. The internet provides a wealth of information that can be helpful in opening up new possibilities to pursue life callings if only the housing budget or tax rates were changed. One useful website, bestplaces.net, is for comparing median home prices and overall cost of living differences.

In summary, your house may be your biggest expense in life. While many guidelines exist for determining what percentage of your income can be devoted to housing, I recommend that you ignore those and work the more relevant question of how much of your life energy you want to be going to housing. You may want to come back to the industry rules at the end of your assessment, but only as a reasonableness test on your thinking and not as a guiding light. As we learned in the housing crash, rules of thumb don't always work and the more responsibility we take for our own decisions the more comfortable we will be with the result.

Cars – I couldn't help but feel a little pride one day when I heard one of my sons telling his friend that he didn't feel the need to own a car to define who he was. To him, a car was just transportation and he defined himself in other ways. Unfortunately, there is a lot of money spent by car manufacturers to convince us that the car we drive does define who we are. Falling for this bait is one more major stumbling block that can hamstring our budget and prevent us from having the freedom we want to pursue our calling in life.

It's important to remember that a new car is not an investment. It depreciates in value- typically as much as 25%-40% in the first two years. One of the smartest moves you might make is let somebody else take this big hit in the first two years and buy the car used.

The internet provides some very useful information to avoid locking ourselves into a bad deal even on a used car. There are a number of good sites, but my favorite is Edmonds.com, Inc. This site has a unique feature that projects the five year cost to own new and used cars. For example, I punched in a 2010 Honda Accord with 50,000 miles on it and it provides the expected cost to own the car over a five year period if driven 15,000 miles a year. The cost breakdown includes: depreciation, taxes and fees, financing (which you can subtract if you pay cash), fuel, insurance, maintenance and repairs. Each year is displayed separately so you can see the expected reduction in depreciation as the car ages, but the corresponding increase in repairs and maintenance. The expected cost of this car over the five year period was $36,826. As you car shop, I would recommend that you use this site to gain perspective on your expected transportation costs. You can also compare the cost of holding onto your existing car and absorbing the higher maintenance costs versus a newer one.

As with housing, I shy away from encouraging you to strictly use formulistic rules on how much to allocate to your transportation budget. I think a husband and wife need to set the priorities together rather than depend on an outside source. However, as a check on your rationale, I would suggest some of the material available on the Crown Ministries website, crown.org. They have a flexible percentage guide to expenses depending on the size of your family and the amount of income you bring home.

Three choices of budgeting: From no sweat to green eye shade detail

Once you have made your choices about some of life's biggest financial decisions, the focus turns to managing the rest of your cash flow to make sure that you are first: living below your means, and second: putting away sufficient savings for your long and short term needs. There is probably an endless variety of ways to accomplish this goal, but I'll share the three that Nancy and I have used successfully at different times in our marriage.

1. **Automated savings plan.** Behavioral economics is an academic discipline that has been blossoming in recent years to challenge traditional economic assumptions about human behavior being rational. For example, it would make perfect sense for families to save diligently for retirement and forgo short term pleasures for long term rewards. But, as we all know, we don't always follow what makes the most sense because we are fallen creatures without perfect knowledge or willpower. One important contribution behavioral economics has brought to personal finance is to suggest that we ought to remove the choice of savings in order to overcome our lack of willpower to diligently save. If we procrastinate about saving for our future goals, then it can make sense to make it automatic so we don't have to think about it each month. In other words, don't give yourself a choice if you are going to save or not, do it automatically.

    The way this budgeting method could work would be to have your payroll department automatically transfer a certain amount of money each month into a savings account just like a portion may already be automatically going into a 401k or IRA. For example, if you make $5,000 a month, you could instruct your payroll department to automatically put $500 in your retirement account and $250 into a savings account to be used for a future need. You now have $4,250 to live on for the rest of the month. As long as you don't borrow extra money on a credit card or rob your savings account, you have successfully lived below your means without tracking exactly where your money went. I admit it's a lazy man's way to budget, but it uses the most powerful force in personal finance- inertia- to force us to live on an agreed upon budget. A fun little book that can help reinforce this basic idea is called *The Richest Man in Babylon*.[xlv] It puts characters and a story around the same idea and is worthy of the short amount of time it will take to read if you need more motivation to do this simple method of budgeting.

2. **The envelope method.** I have found this system works best for people in a real financial crisis. When bill collectors are all calling you, it is sometimes hard to think. Those individuals in a situation like that need to prioritize their needs and allocate whatever money they have coming in to first cover food, shelter and transportation. Only when the storm is over do they need to worry about paying debts and other non-necessities. The envelope method works great to clarify our needs when we're under stress, but is also useful for getting spending under control even when there is no crisis.

The method started back when bills were primarily paid with cash, but the principle still can work today using more modern methods of payment. The first step is to agree on the spending categories for your budget and then set the monthly limit for each category. You will want to add up all the limits you set for each category and make sure that it totals less than you earn each month. For example, you might agree to the following categories and amounts:

Donations	$200
Groceries	$400
Gas	$300
Housing	$1100
Clothes	$75

You would continue this process until you have every expense category covered. Then, if you are paid once a month, you can literally take an envelope and write the expense category on it, for example, "Groceries." Then you would put $400 in the envelope and know that you have to live off of that amount for food for the entire month until you get paid again. At that point, you can start over and replenish the envelope. The advantage of this method is that it forces you to stay in touch with your spending habits because once the money is gone; you are done for the month.

With today's electronic money, some think the cash envelope system is outdated. However, the good news is that you can still do this on hand written worksheets if you keep track of receipts and are diligent to record (subtract) any expenses off of your control sheet. Similarly there are a number of software programs available to help you track your spending electronically in accordance with the envelope system such as "Mvelopes," subscription based service that can be run on mobile apps.

3. **Actual versus budget**. This is the method Nancy and I use today. We discuss every month each category of expenses and agree on what the next 30 day budget will be. Then we are diligent to track everything we buy. At the end of the 30 days we sit down and add it all up and compare what we actually spent to what we budgeted. The advantages are that it also requires serious thought on expenses and tracks actual spending so we're not guessing about our cash outflow. It helps us identify problem areas where we are not in control of our spending and, most important, it enhances our communication and leads to a unity of purpose on our spending plan. The disadvantages are that the budget overages are not always known until after the fact and it does take some commitment to track all spending. However, since we have reached a point in our life where we have a substantial emergency fund, we are not left in a serious bind if we occasionally go over the budget. If we were broke, I would not hesitate to use the envelope system again until we gained some breathing room.

We have used all three of these methods successfully at some point in our marriage. I think all three have their strengths and weaknesses, but in the end, they are all capable of making sure your financial life is not in chaos. If we learn to live below our means with a budget system and a heightened money consciousness, we will be ready for the advanced chapters on dealing with extra money: paying down debt, building wealth and being radically generous.

Summary

Get the big purchases in life right and you will have less pressure to deny yourself lattes and other small pleasures. Developing a communication system that brings unity is at the heart of how to deal with money successfully in marriage. As we successfully manage our expenses below our income, we become ready for the fun part of personal finance: building wealth.

Discussion Questions

1. How important is unity on money in a marriage? How is it best achieved?
2. What are reasons God may be calling you to have children? What are the financial implications? Spiritual implications?
3. What are the pros and cons of having a big house? An expensive car?
4. What budgeting system works best for you?
5. How does a budget complement the Life Energy material in Chapter 5?
6. What do you think you should change about your budget? If married, how closely aligned are you and your spouse on your budget? What changes should you make in communicating on budget priorities
7. Find an accountability partner to meet with you periodically about planned changes.

PART III
Building Wealth

CHAPTER 7

Debt: The Good, the Bad and the Ugly

"Creditors have better memories than debtors."
                                            Benjamin Franklin

"The wicked borrow and do not repay, but the righteous give generously."
                                            Psalm 37:21

Several years ago I had a customer who was getting far behind in her car loan payments. As is standard in the banking industry, we expected car loans to be paid on time. At 10 days past due, you get a written notice. If you are 30 days past due we give you a call and a friendly reminder about your promise to pay on time. As the delinquency gets more severe, the tone of the collection department gets more ominous. This particular lady was approaching 120 days which meant that we were getting ready to repossess her car and we notified her of our intention. Not wanting to lose her car to our collection department, she did the only rational thing she could think of to bring her loan current. She went into the bank down the street, my main competitor, and robbed the bank! Immediately afterwards she came to my bank and paid cash to cover her deficiency. Of course, the police were not far behind and she was quickly apprehended. However, for the moment, her car was safe from being repossessed. Naturally, I gave my competitor a call to thank him for assisting in our collection effort.

Debt- A misunderstood concept

I have a good friend in Illinois who used to call me up on cold days and tell me, "It's colder than a banker's heart out there." He would follow this up with a comment that "it is so cold out there that I saw a banker with his hands in his own pocket!" Of course, since this friend happened to be a lawyer, I would counter with a good lawyer joke to keep him off balance like, "Do you know how a lawyer sleeps? First he lies on one side and then he lies on another."

While the morality of the banking business might be fertile ground for comedy, it is also a serious subject worthy of careful consideration. The ethical question of charging interest on loans has a long and rich history that is beyond the scope of this book. However, because many popular Christian oriented financial advisors take an un-nuanced position against all forms of debt, it is worthy of a short discussion. In fact, the debate over debt has deep roots not only in Christian circles, but in other religions and ancient philosophies as well. Aristotle, for example, condemned all lending with interest because he believed that money could not create wealth by itself.[xlvi] Plato was similarly opposed to lending at interest.[xlvii] Some proponents of Islamic finance make a similar argument.[xlviii] The Roman Catholic Church has a long history of debate over this issue finding in its most recent discussion (1745) that any lending at interest is sin.[xlix]

Debt: The Good, the Bad and the Ugly | 125

So what liberated the Western world from this tradition that all lending at interest is morally wrong? Historians may argue, but I think there is evidence that John Calvin was at the forefront of a revolutionary new understanding that facilitated massive social advancement by liberating Christians from ancient economic thinking on lending. In correspondence sometimes called *"Letter of Advice on Usury,"* Calvin broke new ground in refusing to condemn all lending at interest as usury and opened the door for the possibility of interest for productive purposes as morally acceptable. However, he maintained the church's historic position on condemning lending at interest to the poor.[1] Prior to Calvin, the church simply didn't understand the productive nature of money. He began to rid the stigma of money lending to the non-poor. This change allowed Europe to gain the exponential advances in productivity that come from an economy that approves of financial intermediaries extending credit for productive purposes.

Today the morality of lending is no longer much of an issue. However, that doesn't mean all debt is the same or even morally neutral. In my 36 years of dealing with debt and reading the various biblical comments on usury, I have come to separate debt into three broad categories: **productive, regrettable, and immoral**. I believe those who grasp the differences in the three types of debt and consider what role each might play in achieving their purposes in life are those who are likely to prosper. On the other hand, those who don't understand these concepts and don't use wisdom in our debt culture are likely to end up miserable and confused about how to climb out of a financial mess. Let's consider each type.

Productive Debt

Jim is a pretty typical customer that I have worked with over many years in banking. He's a hard working entrepreneur skilled in construction. Years ago he learned how to build houses working for an experienced home builder, but he wanted to work for himself and he quickly got enough confidence to try to build his first spec house. He and his wife, who made a good income as a dental hygienist, had saved enough money to put 25% down and borrowed the rest through a construction loan. He sold it quickly, making a modest profit and learned enough to continue building new houses with larger profit margins each time.

Jim considered building more and more spec homes, but after studying the rental market, he decided to build his own apartments and become a landlord. Once again, Jim learned from his mistakes on his first effort, but found that he was skilled at building and renting low cost units that cash flowed very nicely over the expenses and loan payments. Jim kept building more units and became more successful with each one. The terms of the loans were usually 25% down and the loans amortized out over roughly 20 years and left enough money after the loan payment, taxes and maintenance for his family to live on.

Jim has now been in the rental business for over 20 years and he is beginning to pay off the loans he used to finance the apartments. He is planning on using the large amount of free cash flow from his apartment buildings for his retirement fund. He is an example of productive debt. He met the housing needs of many low to moderate income families, paid a fair interest rate to the bank, but made far in excess of the bank's rate on his investment.

Some skeptics of productive debt might be saying that Jim just got lucky, but that most people who go into debt for ventures like this end up in the poor house. While it's true that not every loan works out, the odds of success in my experience are very high. In my career as a community banker I have observed that on a percentage basis, only about $2 out of every $1,000 loaned out for

Debt: The Good, the Bad and the Ugly | 127

productive purposes ends up as a debt that is unable to be repaid. The other $998 ends up being repaid after creating wealth for the entrepreneur, the customers served and the bank. My point is that productive debt, when underwritten by professional bankers, usually works out and creates wealth both for the borrower and his or her customers.

The reason the payback ratio is so high for community banks is because we also say "no" to a lot of loan applications. Lots of potential borrowers think that they are onto a terrific idea that if the bank will only finance it, they will pay the loan back and get rich. For example, I usually cringe when somebody wants to start up a new restaurant because they have this great recipe that everyone just loves. Such loans have one of the highest failure rates. Once again, we return to the idea of a "calling" and "purpose" as criteria for a major life decision like borrowing money to start a business. If a borrower is particularly skilled in a line of work, has experience, demonstrated character in the past and has put a significant amount of their own money in the venture, they are likely to find financing for their project. However, when loans are doled out too freely by bankers not skilled in credit analysis to those not apt to pay them back, we can end up with a huge misallocation of resources such as what fed the three trillion dollar bubble in the real estate market leading up to the collapse in 2008.

There is another positive dimension to an economy with risk-taking entrepreneurs borrowing money. The other side of the equation is just as important – the individuals who live below their means and have excess cash to invest who fund these users of debt. Most members of our society are not entrepreneurial, so what do they do with excess cash? Rather than hide it under a mattress, they want to put it to work in a bank, mutual fund or someplace that will earn a return. This excess cash going to fund the latest

I-Phone technology or apartment complex, rather than lying unproductively under the mattress, is the concept John Calvin may have understood, but that philosophers before him could not grasp. Managing our money productively and making it grow is a part of our calling as stewards of God's wealth. We'll discuss investing in more detail later but, generally, the more sophisticated the system of financial intermediaries bringing together those with excess cash with those who have a productive need for it, the more prosperous the country will be.

What is productive debt exactly? It depends. Buying a new piece of equipment that doubles your output would qualify. But what about student loan debt? We will discuss this more at the end of the chapter, but in general, for a doctor who is expected to earn a six figure salary upon graduation, I think the answer is yes, it is wise and productive debt to incur. However, for a liberal arts major to graduate with no reasonable employment opportunities that would provide the resources necessary to pay the debt back, I would counsel to find another way to fund college.

Productive debt should have an expansive definition. It could be for something like a boat loan, or other hobby, if it contributes to the purchaser's ability to relax and return to work more productively. This is assuming it can be absorbed easily in the family budget. Taking on debt can also be productive if the alternative of paying cash means we would have to pay a penalty for an early withdrawal out of a retirement account or pay capital gains taxes if we sell a stock we own. In other words, we might take on some consumer debt to keep our productive assets working for us. Sometimes the classification of debt incurred could be subject to some debate, but usually regrettable debt can be distinguished from productive debt if it creates significant stress on the family budget for something that declines in value. Drop me a note at http://smartmoneywithpurpose.com if you want my opinion on your situation.

Regrettable Debt

We all do things we regret in our lives. I hope you'll not be offended by this term as it's meant as a motivational tool to get it corrected, not to demean those who might have made a mistake in this area. We're all in that camp together. However, I don't think there is a single financial planner anywhere who thinks highly about high interest credit card debt. Rates can go north of 25%. In contrast to the low level of defaults for productive debt, bankers saw more than one in ten credit card loans failing to be repaid in 2010 at the 100 largest banks according to the Federal Reserve Bank of Philadelphia statistics.[li] Past due rates after all the defaults were still over 5%, or one customer in twenty. Just about anyone can get into this type of debt because the rates are so high that the big banks that offer it are able to still make considerable money even with the high default rates.

Therefore, before taking on any type of debt I would encourage you to ask yourself three questions:
1. Is this debt consistent with the concept of being a wise steward? In other words, if you have adopted the premises that we discussed in chapter 2 that God owns it all and we are given the role of managing and making His wealth grow, would He be pleased that you are taking on this debt with His finances?
2. Does this debt support or discourage your ability to achieve your life purpose?
3. Finally, have you calculated the cost of this debt in terms of how many hours of life energy you are spending for the

item being purchased and the interest on the debt? Run the transaction through the decision grid we discussed in Chapter 5 about using life energy before entering into the transaction.

Hopefully those questions will help you make a good decision, but that being said, regrettable debt is not illegal or immoral, it just isn't wise. It's a way to live on more than you make until you run out of credit. The Bible refers to it as bondage: "…the borrower is servant to the lender." Proverbs 22:7. In short, I define regrettable debt as borrowing money to purchase something that probably loses value, does not contribute to growing your productivity and, most important, leaves you stressed out and resentful in trying to pay it back. While credit card loans are easy to beat up on, some car loans may be unwise too. I've seen a lot of strapped income statements that have a high debt to income burden because of the perceived need to drive a $20,000 or more car that is financed when a $5,000 or $10,000 car paid for with cash would work just as well for transportation. There is certainly nothing wrong with driving an expensive vehicle, but if the debt payments bring unneeded stress into your life because of the high percentage of your disposable income it requires, it should be reexamined. Or debt put on a credit card to take a vacation may be productive in the sense that you return to work refreshed, but paying it off at 28% interest over several years puts it into the regrettable debt category. One of the more tense scenes that plays out on the other side of my desk is when a couple comes in to apply for a loan jointly and one of the spouses finds out about hidden credit card debt on the credit bureau report. Now that is really regrettable debt.

Another form of unwise debt is cosigning a loan for a friend or relative without fully expecting to be the one who pays it back. Bankers are pretty smart and if we don't think your friend qualifies for the loan on their own, then there is a good reason for you to assume that you will be responsible for the debt if he defaults. Just say "no" to cosigning. The Scriptures also speak to this ancient practice, "A man lacking in judgment strikes hands in pledge and puts up security for his neighbor." (Proverbs 17:18) This doesn't prohibit us from ever cosigning a loan for someone such as our children to help them get a credit rating, but it does mean we should never do it without the full expectation that we will be the one to service the payments.

Loans on investments that allow an investor to use debt to buy more securities can be a particularly dangerous form of regrettable debt. I have seen very smart investors use margin loans for the purpose of enhancing their investment yield who were almost wiped out because of some unexpected event half way around the world that caused the stock markets to crash. The investment houses that usually make loans on stocks and bonds can force investors to sell their securities at very low prices to pay off this form of debt. If you are considering it, be very, very careful. This form of debt allows you to increase your returns if everything goes right, but also significantly raises your risk and can wipe out your assets if things go very wrong.

We've all made mistakes with our money, so there's no need to beat ourselves up about it if we have too much debt. I think you can classify what portion of your own debts fall into the regrettable category without more attempts by me to define it. The more important question is how do we get out of regrettable debt if we are in it?

I think it's helpful to get angry. You might use the pejorative term "stupid" debt if you want to raise some emotion that the term "regrettable" will not accomplish. If you're content to have a large percentage of your income go to debt payment then you don't have a lot of incentive to drive you to make a change. Change in life is hard and it's okay to get sick and tired of making those credit card payments each month if it results in a resolve to fix it.

Second, take out your frustration to God in prayer about your bondage to regrettable debt. If you are married, it's especially important to strive for a unity of purpose in getting rid of stressful debt as a couple.

The third step is to get a plan. List all your regrettable debt out on a spreadsheet from the lowest balance to the highest balance. So if you have three credit cards with balances of $2,000, $6,000 and $300 plus a car loan for $20,000 you would list them like this:

Bank	Amount	Interest Rate
Citi	$300	22%
Chase	2,000	19%
Discover	6,000	28%
Car	20,000	6%
Total	$28,300	

This plan would have you make minimum payments on all but the lowest balance loan. As you have any extra money, you will apply it to the lowest balance debt to eliminate it as soon as possible. It is psychologically important to be able to cross off a debt as paid. Once the $300 debt is gone, focus on the $2,000 debt until it is gone. You work your way down the ladder in this manner until you are debt free. However, this does not preclude you from trying to sell the car and drive a beater until you are out of debt and can afford to pay cash for a more expensive model.

An alternative to this third step is to pay off the highest interest rate debt first and work your way down to the lowest interest rate. This would be my attack plan, but some need the positive accomplishment to reduce the number of debts as soon as possible. I think either plan is legitimate and is up to you to choose which would motivate you the most.

After agreeing on a plan to attack the debt, the next step is to focus all your energy on execution. This might involve getting an extra job, holding yard sales to sell stuff that can be used to pay down debt and implementing emergency budgeting procedures to eliminate all unnecessary spending as we discussed in chapter 5 and 6. It's doesn't require a high IQ to develop the plan, but it does require a high degree of commitment to carry it out and free yourself of the unnecessary burden.

Immoral Debt

The last type of debt is one that we should not be involved in either as a lender or a borrower. Exodus 28:25 says, "If you lend money to one of my people among you that is needy, do not be like a moneylender; charge him no interest." As Christians, we are to be involved in charity work assisting the poor. We will discuss this more in Chapter 9, but it is clear from the history of the Christian church and Scriptures like this one that God does not want us to take advantage of our neighbor who is destitute by granting loans with interest. People who are truly in need should be shown the hand of grace and not a contract with high interest and a lien on essential collateral. Regrettable debt and productive debt do not fall in these categories, but charitable loans with no interest still have a place in our world. I served on a board for many years that specialized in making micro loans to poor women in Uganda at no interest so they could avoid going into prostitution. Such work is what the Kingdom of God is all about. Five hundred percent interest for a loan to buy groceries is not.

What about Mortgage Debt?

With the tax incentives to purchase a home, I don't counsel many against home ownership because it is usually productive debt, financing an asset that might grow in value. I just caution about how to approach it so that it doesn't become something you regret. First, budget for the worst case scenario. We should all realize that realtors are great people, but they also are paid a commission based on a percentage of the house they sell. Therefore we need to discount the realtor's estimation of how much house we can afford and do our own calculation. If you are a two income marriage, for example, I would suggest that you consider budgeting your house payment on one income. You might have a real budget based on two incomes, but use a shadow plan that would apply if your income were to be cut in half. When my wife and I began to have children, we realized that having her stay home was far more meaningful than the few dollars that we might otherwise have in our budget. We were always very content to live on one salary to have the luxury of raising our children the way we desired. It's a gamble to count on a second salary to make ends meet over a long period of time not knowing if your values will change with children or some other life event.

Other Important Debt Issues

1. **Credit scores.** Millions of people struggle to get loans or low interest loans if their credit score is below 620. If your score is above 760 on the other hand, you are probably getting the best rate available if you need to borrow. So if you are credit score challenged, what are some ways you can fix it? Get a credit card or two if you don't have one. Use it and pay it off each month so you don't end up paying the high

Debt: The Good, the Bad and the Ugly | 135

interest rate. If you can't qualify for a regular card, apply for a secured credit card where the issuing bank gives you a card with a credit line equal to a deposit you make in the bank. Almost anyone can receive this type of credit because the bank doesn't have a risk of default and it will help raise your credit score as you use it and pay it off.

If you already have credit cards with a high balance, the best thing you can do for your credit score is pay it down. Bankers like to see a big difference in the amount you owe and the available credit limits. Getting the balance below 10% really helps.

Bankers also sometimes agree to erase a late payment from your credit history for good customers. Make the request in writing as it never hurts to ask and it could make a big difference in your credit score

Adding a small installment loan, such as an auto loan, to your credit history can also help if you pay it off on time.

While some debt averse financial counselors scoff at worrying about your credit score, the reality is that it is important. Even some jobs and insurance rates are dependent on maintaining a good credit rating and we should take advantage of the opportunity to maintain a high score through diligently paying our bills on time.

2. **Medical debt.** We never know when we will be hit with an unexpected health event that results in large unexpected

medical bills. If you can't pay the entire balance, work out a plan that you can afford with the hospital or doctor. However, be sure to ask about debt discounts or forgiveness programs before agreeing to a workout plan. Many hospitals have programs that forgive millions of dollars a year. Discounts for paying off amounts owed are also common, and many times all you need to do is inquire about them. Depending on your situation you may be able to pay off your obligation for pennies on the dollar.

3. **Strategic Default.** This is a new term that has been used in the last few years. It refers to an idea promoted by some financial planners to simply walk away from a mortgage loan that is higher than the value of the property used as collateral even if you have the means to keep paying on the loan. The logic is that while it might impact your credit score for a few years, you will be far better off in the long run than continuing to pay on the loan.

When I meet with individuals considering this strategy who are Christians, I usually ask them if they are familiar with the third commandment: "You shall not misuse the name of the Lord your God."(Ex 20:7) What does that mean? Certainly more than just swearing in God's name. When we are baptized we take the name of Christ on ourselves, all our actions reflect to the world what Jesus is really like. As we talk, most realize that the document that is signed for a loan states, "I promise to pay..." As a Christian, we have a duty to not walk away from our commitment but to let our "yes be yes," even though we might be better off financially if we hired a lawyer to help us evade our obligation. As Psalm 37:21 states it is "the wicked that borrow and do not repay." This modern day legal maneuver may be popular, but as a follower of Jesus it is not the right thing to do if you have the ability to repay.

4. **Bankruptcy.** Regrettably, sometimes in spite of our best efforts, the only way out of a financial situation is to file bankruptcy. I am most compassionate in seeing this strategy as legitimate when I see someone who becomes sick and has lost their ability to earn money. When there is no prospect of earning money due to poor health, the bills are unlikely to get paid. Or, sometimes the best laid business plans fail and the owner has no recourse but to file for bankruptcy protection. That's part of our capitalistic system where we have the freedom to succeed, but also the ability to fail. Divorce is also a great destroyer of wealth and sometimes when we face an emotional and financial hurricane like that in our lives we are left with few alternatives. In short, while there is abuse of this method of having debts discharged, it is also a moral option at times for some who have done all they can to pay their bills, but still come up short. When considering this option it is usually a good idea to involve spiritual counselors who you trust to help evaluate your situation objectively because of the ease of deceiving ourselves into taking this course without exhausting other options. Additionally, it is a good idea to practice full transparency with your creditor about your situation. Most banks will work through a situation with a troubled loan customer to try to find a plan that is reasonable based

on the circumstances. This may include reduced interest rates or even loan principle write downs. Most lenders will work with a troubled borrower to develop a workout plan as opposed to the alternative of forcing a customer into bankruptcy. It's not a pleasant time for those who have extreme financial trouble, but it does allow the true character of the individual to be revealed in how they respond to the difficult circumstances.

5. **Student Loan Debt.** I list student loan debt after bankruptcy because it will usually not be discharged through that process. I believe it is one of the most dangerous forms of debt because it is so easy to get into, and very few schools are helping students to evaluate their ability to repay it. Countless individuals have very sad stories about how they got into student loan debt to earn degrees that did not have the earning power to service the student loan debt. In many ways it has parallels to the real estate bubble where borrowers were given loans without evaluating the capacity to repay the debt. Since it cannot be discharged in bankruptcy, it can significantly upset lives. Currently the average undergraduate is leaving school with $29,400 of debt.[liii] Therefore many graduates are forced to put off their plans and are living with their parents rather than launching into the life they desire. I am not opposed to all student loan debt as I've seen many professionals, for example, graduate with significant debt that was easily serviced. However, I strongly encourage you to think carefully about what your likely earnings will be upon graduation and calculate what percentage of that income you will be comfortable paying out in student loan debt payments.

Summary

Debt has a long and colorful history of debate in the Christian church. However, since the Reformation, it has been less controversial. As a banker and student of the Scriptures for the last 36 years, I have become convinced that there are three types of debt: productive, regrettable and immoral. All debt must be used judiciously, but regrettable debt is best paid off with a focused effort and immoral debt should be avoided by all. Productive debt benefits all of us and leads to excess cash flow that can be used for investments which we will discuss in the next chapter.

Discussion Questions

1. What are examples of productive debt? How does it contribute to wealth generation in a society?
2. What are examples of regrettable debt? How does it destroy our wealth?
3. Why is some debt immoral? What form does it take in the United States?
4. List your debt, if you have any, and develop a plan to pay off any regrettable or immoral debt. What are action items you can take to stay focused on the plan?
5. What would be a proper use of debt that helps you fulfill your purpose in life?

CHAPTER 8

9 Habits of Successful Investing

Rule # 1: Never Lose Money
Rule # 2: Never forget rule number 1.
                                    Warren Buffett

"I can calculate the movement of stars, but not the madness of men."
                                    Sir Isaac Newton

Divide your portion to seven, or even to eight, for you do not know what misfortune may occur on this earth.
                                    Ecclesiastes 11:2

Since Warren Buffett began Berkshire Hathaway in 1965, his company has had a compounded annual gain of 19.7% and an overall gain of 693,518% through the end of 2013.[liii] In other words, according to the Berkshire Hathaway annual report, if you had invested $19.00 in his company 49 years ago, your investment would be worth $134,973 today. How much would you have if you'd put in $1,000? I'll let you do the math, but trust me, it's a lot. It's easier to understand just how brilliant Buffett has been if you compare his results to the broader stock market, such as the S&P 500 index of stocks. The S&P had a very respectable annual compounded gain of 9.8% over that same time period and an overall gain of 9,841%. But, that same $19.00 would only be worth about $1,854 today if it had been invested in the S&P index. Or, if that same $19.00 had been conservatively invested at a 5% rate it would now be valued at only about $207.50. It's not surprising that Buffett, now in his 80's, draws crowds of more than 30,000 at his annual meeting that is called, "The Woodstock of Capitalism," where investors hang onto his every word.

Sir Isaac Newton was one of the greatest minds of the second millennium. He discovered gravitational force and established the three universal laws of motion. Without his contributions, we would probably never have been able to explore space beyond our atmosphere. I always struggled with calculus in school, but Newton is credited as one of the two primary creators of that discipline. I could go on, but I'm sure I don't need to because he is a mythic figure in Western culture. However, what you might not know is that for all his accomplishments in the world of science, he lost his shirt as an investor. Sir Isaac got burned in a big way by investing in South Sea shares. In the second half of 1720 Newton's holdings lost 20,000 pounds.[liv] This would be about $4,000,000 to $5,000,000 in today's dollars. It is no wonder he is attributed with the quote, "I can calculate the movement of the stars, but not the madness of men." His investment in South Sea was a loss he never fully recovered from. The unique gifts that Sir Isaac displayed in science were not transferrable to the world of investing.

This game of investing is a full contact sport where we can win and create wealth, but even the professionals can suffer staggering losses in a short time. Humility and caution are in order.

9 Habits of Successful Investing

As with all the other topics in this book, I believe investing should also be guided by purpose and stewardship. I've distilled what I've found to be some keys to success in managing our excess cash flow in the context of a Christian worldview in these nine habits. However, this is a vast and complex topic that can't be adequately covered in one chapter. I will give you the basics, but I'll also list some suggested sources on smartmoneywithpurpose.com for those of you who might want to go deeper. However, this chapter is not intended to be an investment guide and you should consult competent professionals on your financial plan.

Habit 1: Invest in Your Calling First

In 1984 I invested $1,000 in a CPA review course. My wife and I didn't have much money at the time, but I felt that it was important to gain that designation for my career in the banking business. After a lot of work and successfully completing the exam I was able to leverage passing that test to obtain three job offers at substantially higher salaries. My own employer countered in order to keep me and I received a $10,000 raise and promises of more to come. The immediate return on my $1,000 investment was 1,000%. Not a bad return, but a better way to look at the return on that investment was that it increased my base salary not for just one year, but for the next 30 years and counting. Ignoring compounding, that $1,000 investment in my calling has now returned 30,000% or $300,000.

This principle is easily taught to teenagers with a simple lawn mowing business. Buying a reliable lawn mower for $400 should last for several seasons if well cared for. Picking up just a few yards to mow will quickly pay for the capital expense and begin to throw off terrific returns on the investment. Say your son or daughter picks up five lawns to mow at $35.00 each. Let's assume the season lasts for

15 weekly mowing jobs. That means total revenue for one season would be $2,625.00 less gas and oil of say, $625.00 for a net profit of $2,000. The initial investment is paid for and the return on the investment is 500%...in one year. Not even Warren Buffett can make that kind of return! Of course, a bit of time and effort is involved, but for a young teenager, that is a terrific investment that he couldn't find anywhere in the stock market. This is one reason why my wife and I have always encouraged our kids to learn the principles of entrepreneurship in having their own lawn mowing business.

The point to all of this is that before you begin to worry about putting money into the stock or bond market, you need to exhaust the opportunities you have to improve upon the skills connected to your life purpose. You will eventually run out of opportunities to invest in your own skills, but we should realize that while they last there will usually never be a better opportunity for high returns than when we invest in ourselves.

Habit 2: Use Investing Lessons from the Science of Hitting

Ted Williams was the man who wrote the book on hitting a baseball—literally. According to Williams in *The Science of Hitting*[lv] the hardest thing to do in baseball is hit the ball. Never having been able to hit a curve ball, I tend to agree with him. And he should know since he was the last person to hit over .400 in a season, hitting .406 in 1941. In his book, he had a grid of 77 little zones in the strike zone. He said that if he only swung at the balls in a particular area of the strike zone he would bat over .400. If he swung at balls on the outside corner, but still in the strike zone, he would bat .225. So his philosophy was all about waiting for the right pitch that is in your sweet spot before swinging.

In baseball, you can get called out on strikes if you never swing at a pitch that is outside your sweet spot, but in investing, you never have to swing until you see an investment that you understand. Warren Buffett, for example, won't invest in tech stocks because they are outside of his sweet spot. He talks about Ted Williams hitting philosophy in investing terms, "In investments, there's no such thing as a called strike. You can stand there at the plate and the pitcher can throw the ball right down the middle, and if it's General Motors at $47 and you don't know enough to decide General Motors at $47, you let it go right on by and no one's going to call a strike. The only way you can have a strike is to swing and miss."[lvi] We all have a circle of competence, and the great thing about investing is you only have to do it a few times to make a big difference.

Let's make this practical and assume that you and I both become aware of a rental house that is going to be sold. I have no particular expertise in buying and managing rental houses, but it seems like a good buy from what the realtor is telling me. You on the other hand have managed rental properties for years, know the market prices and have construction experience that helps you evaluate the quality of the home. Which one of us is more likely to overpay for the investment? If I buy this house and it is a successful investment, it is not because I was wise. Even bad hitters sometimes connect when the ball is out of their sweet spot. But, I should pass on the opportunity because the odds are not in my favor. I should look for something more in my circle of competence. You, on the other hand, may feel very comfortable making this purchase because you know that price is well under what its true value is as a rental property and you know how to make improvements that will improve the cash flow.

In the 1980's, I was in Houston when Texaco and Pennzoil were locked in a fierce court battle. I wouldn't have had a clue who was going to win, but I met a lawyer who was following the case very closely. He was convinced that Pennzoil would win a big verdict. He took all the money he could gather and bought stock options on Pennzoil. As it turned out, Pennzoil won a multibillion dollar verdict and his stock options went through the roof. Congratulations to this guy who saw a hanging curve ball coming right down the middle of his area of expertise and he hit it out of the ball park. If I had tried to invest in that court case I probably would have bought Texaco because I had no expertise in it. God gives us each unique circles of competence that we can use to gain an edge in investing.

In other words, we all should stay within our own sweet spot when making investments. I have seen many smart people make very dumb financial investments because they made the mistake of thinking their excellence in one field will transfer to other investments. For example, doctors and lawyers are very smart in their sphere, but I have seen some of my best customers in those fields be prone to make very poor decisions in investing. They fail to understand that their brilliance in medicine or the law does not necessarily translate into investing outside of their profession. So before you make any investment, ask yourself why you think you are smarter than the person on the other end of the transaction selling the stock, bond or other investment. I like to visualize the seller before any investment I make. I assume that the seller is a sophisticated hedge fund manager who is a lot smarter than me who must have a good reason for getting out of it. That dose of humility can give us pause to avoid making a bad move, or it can give us assurance that we really do have a gift for investing in this particular area.

Habit 3: Use "Purpose Buckets" to Stay the Course without Panicking

Every dollar you retain should have a purpose attached to it. The vain accumulation of money only for the sake of accumulation will lead to idolatry as we have discussed. However, the power of a purpose-focused investment plan is not only a useful technique in guarding against this spiritual problem; it also leads to less stress in your financial life as well as a wise allocation of your resources. Let me explain the bucket approach.

First, think about the various purposes for money in your life. I always recommend that you have an emergency fund bucket where you keep six to eight months of your living expenses. You might have a second bucket where you keep money saved for another car. A third bucket might be a vacation fund. These buckets should be unique to you, but others might include a bucket for starting a new business someday, a college education bucket, wedding bucket, a retirement bucket and a sabbatical bucket.

After identifying the purpose buckets in your life, you need to make a determination of when you will need the funds in each bucket. For example, the emergency fund needs to be available almost immediately for when the water heater blows up unexpectedly or your son accidently puts a baseball through the neighbor's window. The new car bucket on the other hand might be five years away from being needed. The vacation bucket is likely going to be needed within 12 months, the new business bucket might be a ten year dream, college fifteen years away and retirement 35 years from now. Investments with a compatible time horizon can then be used to fill the buckets.

The implications of thinking about your finances in this way are to give you the freedom to act prudently. For example, you might fill the long term buckets with investments that have the highest growth potential over many years such as stocks or real estate, even though they might be volatile and risky in the short term. One of the biggest mistakes novice investors can make is to panic when the markets go down and sell low, only to panic that they are missing out when the markets go back up and buying high. Realizing that you don't need to worry about short term market gyrations for long term bucket goals will make us calmer and wiser investors who buy low and sell high. On the other hand, with this system, we keep our short term buckets filled with safe, liquid investments that don't fluctuate in value because we will need them shortly. Let me illustrate how this system works with a 30 year old couple who have two children and $100,000 of investable assets. Here's how their buckets might look:

Bucket	Value	Investments Used	Time Horizon
Emergency	$20,000	Bank savings account	Immediate
Vacation	$3,000	Money Market fund	6 months
Car	$6,000	Short term bond fund	3 years
Business	$20,000	70% stocks/30% bonds	10 years
College	$8,000	80% stocks/20% bonds	15 years
Retirement	$43,000	90% stocks/10% real estate	35 years

This family has adequate resources to deal with the short term problems that might surface with their short term buckets well stocked. This structure then allows them to basically ignore the stock market when it takes a sudden dive because those stock investments are all in long term buckets that will likely perform just fine over the long term. It's an understandable system that takes the stress and the purposelessness out of investing.

Habit 4: Diversify to Preserve and Grow Wealth

I had lunch with Jack a few years ago before the financial crises. He was a small business man who had sold his company at a good time, and he had received a couple of million dollars of stock in the acquiring corporation. It was a windfall that could have been a life changer. Rather than diversify his concentration of wealth in that one stock, he felt comfortable holding 90% of his net worth in that company that seemed to be doing well and was paying a good dividend. Then the financial crises hit and his stock lost over 90% of its value. Jack had ignored a Biblical principle of diversification from Ecclesiastes 11:2 which advises splitting our wealth into seven or eight different portions.

To be fair, concentration of our wealth is sometimes a good thing. Many farmers have a huge concentration of wealth in their farms. They are passionate about what they do and willing to bear the risks of having all their eggs in one basket. Business owners who are passionate about their business see no need to diversify their wealth as they have a calling and understand the risks of their chosen profession. In fact, the greatest wealth is created by successful concentration of assets as seen in many examples like Bill Gates and Microsoft stock, Sam Walton and Wal-Mart stock or, John D. Rockefeller and Standard Oil. None of these individuals diversified much through the building of their great wealth. However, they are the exception and not the rule. Most of us do not own businesses that continue to need reinvestment for growth. We are more concerned about having sufficient resources to meet our life goals. Diversification is generally the way to go for those of us who want to grow and protect our wealth as good stewards of what God has given us. But the first rule of diversification is to understand that it guarantees that you will not earn the highest possible return because you will have some money in lagging investments.

Entire textbooks are written about this topic, sometimes referred to as Modern Portfolio Theory, which is a mathematical expression of the concept of diversification in investing. We'll barely scratch the surface, but the basic principal of diversification in non-financial language is that you want some investments that zig when everything else zags. For example in the 2000 to 2002 time period we saw the US stock market collapse, dropping about 50%. However, bonds posted good gains along with real estate investment trusts. When some sectors are sinking others are likely soaring thus smoothing out your overall portfolio. This reduction in volatility can be reassuring, especially if we are on the verge of a big change in life such as retiring.

This area of managing our investments is complex and if you don't want to have to spend a lot of time thinking about where to diversify your portfolio, you should consider hiring a competent investment advisor to assist with this part of your stewardship. They should be able to show you expected returns for each mix of asset classes and explain the mathematical expectations that normally exist around the targeted return. You should also understand the worst case returns for the asset allocation that you chose. For others, life cycle funds have been a relatively new vehicle that is advertised to change your level of investments to get less risky automatically the older you get. Whether you DIY or hire it out, it is necessary to rebalance at least once a year to the targeted percentage of investments.

I'll give you a personal example that has a few more moving parts. I've listed below roughly how my wife and I targeted our diversification strategy going into the Great Recession for our long term buckets. While it weathered the downturn fairly well for us, it is not intended for specific use as everyone has a unique financial situation, goals and purposes. However, it gives you an idea of how

9 Habits of Successful Investing | 151

a diversification strategy might look and how I perceive the risk and volatility. Once we set this program up, we usually rebalance about once a year so the time committed is minimal.

Cash 10% (CD's) Very low risk and volatility
Insurance Products 10%
    Fixed annuities 5% Very low risk and volatility
    Cash value life 5% Very low risk and volatility
Bonds 30%
    I-bonds and TIPS 10% (Inflation protected bonds) Very low risk and volatility
    US investment grade 5% Moderate risk and volatility
    US high yield bonds 5% High risk and volatility
    Investment grade foreign bonds 5% Moderate risk and volatility
    Emerging market bonds 5% High risk and volatility
Stocks 35%
    Large US 15% Moderate risk and volatility
    Mid cap US 5% High risk and volatility
    Small cap US 5% High risk and volatility
    Emerging markets 5% High risk and volatility
    Developed markets 5% High risk and volatility
Real Estate (Not including personal residence) 10% High risk and volatility
Commodities 5% High risk and volatility

Your assignment, whether you DIY or not, is to write down what percentage of your portfolio by buckets you want invested in different sectors. If this is all Greek to you, you should find a financial advisor with a teachable heart that can help come up with a plan for you. If she is good, she will make sure you understand the risks of the allocations. This simple act is very powerful. Your written allocation plan can be a roadmap for you and a reminder that when markets go down, and your confidence waivers, that you put the strategy in place in a less emotional moment. That written plan should bring peace to you even when the markets have high turbulence.

Habit 5: Trick, Cajole or Force Yourself to Save, Save, Save

I've worked with a lot of people who started out with nothing and became wealthy over time through diligently saving. However, I've only read about people like Warren Buffett that became wealthy because they were such smart investors. If I have to choose between the two in a bet, I'd take the diligent savers every time over the smart investors.

If there are so many good reasons to save, why do we struggle with it? Over my years in management I would always point out to my employees the rationale for the 401(k) match, for example. And yet, even with the tax advantages and the great immediate return from the company match, many employees would decline the benefit. (Prevailing wisdom is that unfortunately we are just not wired for delayed gratification.) Moreover, we all know that the earlier we start saving the more wealth we generate in the long run to say nothing of the peace of mind we enjoy.

Let's take a lesson from the behavioral psychologists who encourage us to make savings automatic so we don't have to make a decision each time. We should normally take advantage of any company match in our retirement program by having automatic deductions each pay period. We might kick our mortgage payment up an extra $100 automatically each month for example. Or, create rules like, "we will save any income tax refund," or, "any overtime pay or half of any bonuses will be saved immediately." And in addition we need to mentally declare our savings and brokerage accounts, and especially retirement funds, as "off limits" for meeting current bills. At the same time, we should make sure that we don't fool ourselves into saving by these methods while at the same time racking up credit card debt to satisfy the immediate consumption urge.

If you want to see your savings grow faster, forget about concentrating on home run investments and focus on increasing your savings by setting up automatic processes you don't have to think about.

Habit 6: Manage the Subtractions in Investing

Having managed investment advisors for much of my career, I know that most of them are ethical and good at offering wealth management services. But, as in every profession, there are those who might seek to exploit their knowledge by putting their interests ahead of yours. More likely still is that you might carelessly chase the latest high performing mutual fund without being aware of the costs that could reduce your savings significantly over time. Let me give you an example.

Assume that two investors put $10,000 in separate mutual funds and left them there to compound over 50 years. The yields of the investments were the same, averaging 8% over the 50 year time period. How much would their investment be worth? Investor A put his money in a mutual fund that had a 2.5% management fee each year while investor B used an index fund that only charged .07%. The value of investor A's fund was $145,400 in year 50 while Investor B had a balance of $453,560. A difference of over $308,000. Expenses matter. While the general level of fund expenses is coming down, there are still significant differences for basically the same service. As good stewards, it is up to us to understand what fees are being charged and what we are receiving for it. Index and mutual fund expenses are public information and you should spend the time to find out the cost of holding your funds in these investment vehicles before committing money to them.

But some in the financial services industry will object to this line of thinking by saying that we shouldn't care how much the fees are if the total performance turns out to be better with the higher fees. In other words, don't you get what you pay for in the end? Isn't it worth it to pay higher fees if the performance more than compensates for the cost? I cannot argue with the logic, but the reality is that the higher costs almost never result in better performance. Even big institutional investors sometimes fall for this faulty argument. The Wall Street Journal ran an article reporting on a study done by the Maryland Public Policy Institute and the Maryland Tax Education Foundation that had compared public-employee pension plans.[lvii] The findings were that the 10 states that paid the highest in money management fees had lower investment performance than the 10 states that paid the lowest fees. If the large institutional pensions are unable to justify the high fees that come from the very best hedge funds in the world compared to low cost index funds, then doesn't it make sense that individual investors like us are also better off focusing on finding low cost funds? Many other studies have validated that holding passive low cost index funds that don't try to outperform the market consistently outperform actively managed funds with higher costs.

Warren Buffett, for example, made a bet in 2008 against a hedge fund called Protégé Partners. The bet was fairly simple. Protégé Partners could pick a group of hedge funds to perform against a simple S&P 500 index fund over the course of 10 years. Buffett bet $1 million that they couldn't outperform the simple index. As of early 2014, the hedge funds have returned just 12.5% while the S&P 500 is up 43.8%.[lviii] In other words, the investing world is one place where you don't get what you pay for.

Taxes are a similar drag on investment results. Frequent trading usually results in tax bills that can significantly reduce your overall yield. Many mutual funds and ETF's (exchange traded funds) offer tax advantaged trading that can limit the friction of having to pay taxes on your investments until compounding has had the chance to work its wonderful magic. You should discuss the tax consequences of your investments with a knowledgeable advisor if you are not familiar with the nuances of tax regulations.

Additionally, be wise about the incentives your financial advisor might have to put you in an inappropriate investment. The Wall Street Journal ran an article that discussed offers being made to financial advisors that would reward them with a Maserati if they could sell $7.5 million in annuities in 2014 and a BMW, Range Rover or Porsche for selling at least $6 million.[lix] These annuities, by the way, paid the advisor a 9% commission for whatever they sold in addition to the cars. Could awarding advisors Maseratis and 9% commissions influence their judgment? I think we all know the answer to that. Be wise.

But I would not want anyone to read this chapter and think that it is never appropriate to pay for financial advice. Many people need financial advice and it can be well worth the cost. For example, one of the classic mistakes individual investors make is to buy when stock prices are high and sell when they are low. If you have a financial advisor that is willing to help you hang on during the downturns, she is well worth the fee she might be charging. Additionally, many of us need help keeping up with the latest financial innovations in the markets. Either we don't have time to study topics like asset diversification or we can't understand these complex topics. In those cases the money paid to a financial advisor can be well worth the alternative of keeping our money invested in inappropriate investments.

Habit 7: Embrace Humility

There will always be investing hot shots like Warren Buffett. You and I are not them. And the quicker we understand that the sooner we can begin to grow our wealth. I've forgotten this lesson many times and become convinced that I was able to see an investing gem that no one else was seeing. More times than not, I was humbled to find out that I was missing something that others were seeing.

So when you are contemplating a big investment bet, remember that the market is generally an efficient mechanism that already reflects the value of the stock. You probably don't have access to the latest market research or insider tip, so temper your enthusiasm before pulling the trigger and losing some valuable capital. Proverbs 16:18 is a verse we should all keep in mind when it comes to being confident in our investing prowess, "Pride goes before a fall."

Habit 8: The Longer Term Your Investing Horizon, the Better Your Decision

My fear for those coming into money because of following the principles in this book is that they will begin watching business channels. They have pundits every hour shouting that you should be buying or selling because of some overpowering reason. Let me quote my favorite investor, Warren Buffett, from his 2014 annual report: "Forming macro opinions or listening to the macro or market predictions of others is a waste of time. Indeed, it is dangerous because it may blur your vision of the facts that are truly important. When I hear TV commentators glibly opine on what the market will do next, I am reminded of Mickey Mantle's scathing comment: "You don't know how easy this game is until you get into that broadcasting booth."[lx]

Many people are scared of the stock market because they either lost money in it or have heard about others losing money. If you don't understand something, it's good not to buy into it. However, for the rational, calm investor who knows facts such as that the Dow Jones Industrial Index advanced from 66 to 11,497 plus a rising stream of dividends in the 20th century, it's possible to ignore the day to day market gyrations and stay focused on the long term goals and the long term trends of increasing shareholder value for patient investors."[lxi] I believe over the long term, investing in the stock market is a wise course. But if you are going to panic every time the market goes through a cyclical downturn, then you probably should just stay away from it.

Consider children for example. They make almost no sense economically in the short run. They will absorb our time, treasure, and talents for many years without any economic benefits. However, we all know that they hold the key to the future prosperity of a society. Therefore, we invest heavily in them, not because we expect a short term dividend, but because we know that they hold the potential to change our world for good many years down the road. In fact, I think the Bible hints at this long term view of how we ought to think about our stewardship regarding children in verses such as the second commandment that assures us that he will "show mercy to thousands of generations of them that love me and keep my commandments." In my experience, the longer our investment horizon, the better our stewardship will be.

Habit 9: Invest Ethically

Some see investing as devoid of any consideration of the ethics of the products or services being sold. The goal, they would say, is to maximize your return on investment and as long as it is legal, you should not be concerned with the morality of the company. For a follower of Christ, I don't believe that investing philosophy is an option.

If we are serious about all of life being an act of stewardship for the furtherance of God's kingdom, we must consider our investments as part of that responsibility. Like the limited restraints God put on Adam and Eve in the garden to enjoy all that creation had to offer, except abstaining from one tree, so we too have an almost unlimited number of legitimate choices in investing that are part of taking dominion over the earth. However, there are some businesses that are working at odds with the goals of God's kingdom that we should avoid even if it means failing to maximize our returns.

I believe that the companies to be avoided will be different for each of us depending on our ethical framework. I think what's important is to follow the dictates of our conscience in investing so that whatever we do, we do it in faith with a clean conscious. For example, I can't in good conscience invest in the gambling or pornography industries because of how I see them corrupting our work ethic and causing family problems with the growing addiction problems in these areas.

Each of us should take seriously our call to use our resources wisely for God's glory. However, I don't think that this excludes us from using widely held index funds that may have a tiny fraction of their total stock holdings in an industry we object too. While we should strive to purify our investments to reflect our values, we may not be able to achieve total purity given our inability to find the perfect mutual fund or ETF that fully reflects our Christian sensibilities. However, we should all make a good faith effort to align our investments, as much as possible, with a Biblical worldview without getting legalistic and trying to achieve the impossible given the limitations of current mutual and index funds offerings.

Further Study

We have covered a lot of topics on a very complex subject in this chapter. I would encourage you to also look at the resources I list for further study at http://smartmoneywithpurpose.com.

Summary

Investing is just one more area of life that falls under the Lordship of Christ for the believer. Besides the need to be a faithful steward over the wealth God has allowed us to manage, we should also be structuring our investments according to the likely needs we will have in achieving our life purposes.

Discussion Questions

1. Evaluate your investment opportunities in your calling. Where can you invest more money to make you better at what you do in life? Is there a potential return from additional investment?
2. What are your circles of competence where you should have a significant advantage over others to gain insight on potential investments?
3. Being honest, what mistakes have you made in the past in making investments?
4. Think about your purposes in life and draw out as many purpose "buckets" as you can think of that would make sense for your financial planning. What are the appropriate time horizons for each bucket and what types of investments make sense for each?
5. Given your calling in life, does it make sense for you to have your wealth concentrated or diversified? Why? If you conclude that you should be diversified, map out a diversification plan for your family.
6. Why does it make sense to automate your savings? If you're not satisfied with your current savings plan, what changes will you make?
7. If you have investments, research them and determine how much of your investments are going to fund expenses. Calculate how much these expenses will subtract from your net worth over a twenty year period.
8. Have you considered investments from an ethical perspective in the past? How might you make changes to make sure your investments contribute to a world that is more reflective of a Christian society?

CHAPTER 9

Joyful Generosity

Place the basket before him. And you and the Levites and the aliens among you shall rejoice in all the good things the Lord your God has given to you and your household.
                                            Deuteronomy 26: 11

"God loves a cheerful giver."
                                            II Corinthians 9:7

I have a dog named Butkus. He's a tough looking little guy, half pug and half beagle. What I love most about Butkus is his uninhibited expression of joy when I come home at night. If I sneak in the door and he doesn't hear me I will yell, "Yo, Butkus!" and then all pandemonium breaks loose. He comes running and leaps in the air at me while at the same time letting out the most joyful little whelps that a dog can make. I only encourage him by grabbing his blanket to start a tug of war fight with him that will go on as long as I have fight left in me. Having raised five children in a disciplined environment, it's somewhat embarrassing to now have a dog that is totally out of control, but I have not yet been able to bring myself to squelch that expression of pure joy he shows every night to his master. It's a daily reminder of what joy really looks like.

You might imagine Butkus flying through the air in joyful flight, but if a book could sing, this is also where I would have you hearing Beethoven's music put to "Joyful, Joyful We Adore Thee." Such joyous Christmas music should set the tone for any discussion of generosity. If charitable giving is not rooted in the joy of living a life that is conscious of what God has done for us, then it will in the end be corrupted by some poor motive or be extinguished altogether.

Take my friend Al. I first met him when he called our church and said he was moving into our area to take a new job at a manufacturing plant and he needed some help unloading his truck. While Al was a smart guy and well versed in the Scripture, almost immediately it became apparent that his family life was pretty miserable and driven by a lot of issues, not the least of which was his refusal to relax his grip on his money. Kids who left a light on when they left a room were severely chastened. Any questionable spending by his wife resulted in a major confrontation. Giving to the church was rare. It wasn't that they were broke. They had plenty of money to live on, but the obsessive pinching of pennies left their marriage and family life devoid of joy. In the end, the marriage ended in divorce and he is now estranged from his children. Joylessness is a serious sin.

So how do we find the right balance with money between wise frugality and a joyful celebration of life characterized by a generous spirit? I found a clue to this maze years ago when somebody gave me a book titled, *Tithing and Dominion*.[lxii] I don't remember much about that book except for the examination of the three types of tithes found in the Old Testament: the rejoicing tithe, the poor tithe and the Levitical tithe. *I didn't even know that there was more than one tithe before reading the book,* but I found in this biblical wisdom a life changing view of money that has brought a lot of joy and balance to my family's life. If you have never looked deeply at the Bible's view of generosity, I think the place to start is in discovering the principles laid out for generosity before Jesus was born in these three Tithes. They go together to form a wonderful balance in life that contributes to Shalom-or wellness-in our lives and in the lives of those around us. Only after understanding the foundation in the Old Testament can we then build on those principles with the wisdom of the New Testament.

The Rejoicing Tithe

I'm not a theologian, so I'm not going to drill down into the minutia of these tithes. However, I think the broad principles are still applicable to us today and easy to understand since Jesus endorsed tithing in a backhanded compliment to the Pharisees in Matthew 23:23. Let's start with the rejoicing tithe because joy is not a small matter with God. For us to see our calling in Christ as one of misery and distress is a denial of Christ. Rather, for us to see our calling as one of "love, joy, peace, longsuffering, gentleness, goodness, faith, meekness, and self control" (Galatians 5:22-23) and "joy unspeakable" (I Peter 1:18) is to confirm that Christ has come into a broken world to heal it. Therefore, it still makes sense that we ought to be using a part of our money to rejoice before Him with praise and feasting as occurred in the Old Testament days. "You shall rejoice in your feast." (Deut 16:14).

Some of the particular passages that reference the rejoicing tithe include Deut 12:14-19, 14: 22-27 and 26: 10-11. These verses make it clear that one purpose of the tithe was to party before God. Fine drinks, rich meats and bread consumed before God in time of rejoicing and sharing with others were a part of this tithe.

In essence, it was meant to make the heart glad because of what God has done for us.

I believe that this emphasis on rejoicing (Lev 23:33-43) is critical to those of us who are naturally savers. I can get caught up in my savings goals and exclude other necessities if I don't have a constraint to remember that God wants us to live full lives even when we may not be meeting our long term goals. This balance in life is particularly important when raising children. I've often thought that it is not a mistake that one of the qualifications for an elder is that his children be believers. If we raise our kids in a joyless family environment that never relaxes the grip on money to rejoice in what the Lord has done, then why should we expect them to follow us in our Christian faith when they grow up? The attractiveness of the Christian life ought to be most evident to those closest to us and that can only happen if monetary resources are a part of creating a celebratory environment in the home around God's redemption of all things.

But what does this look like in real life? A strict interpretation of rejoicing tithe passages like the ones in Deuteronomy would lead us to allocate 10% of our increase each year to rejoicing. I'm not comfortable saying that amount is still required for us today, but it clearly is a good idea to have a rejoicing line item in your budget. My wife and I have practiced a variety of methods of spending the rejoicing tithe in our lives. We have invited friends out to dinner and made it clear to them that this meal is a part of our rejoicing over God's work in our lives. We have gotten some quizzical looks, but it usually leads to some interesting dinner conversation about the whole concept of planning to rejoice in our lives. Vacations can be a part of this tithe as we rest from our work to celebrate God's provision in our life. We have also used this portion of our budget to attend Christian family camps and conferences in which we are able to relax and fellowship with like-minded believers. You can be creative, but a failure to budget for joyful celebrations and to practice rejoicing is contrary to Biblical wisdom in using money. It is also a good antidote to those of us who feel guilty if we are spending money enjoying the blessings that God has put into our life.

Practical Suggestion: What does practicing the "rejoicing tithe" look like in the 21s century? Let me give you a Montana example. Let's assume that you just received a $2,000 bonus and you're wondering what you should do with it. You agree with your spouse to allocate $200 of the bonus for rejoicing in God's provision for your family of four. You let the kids know that God has blessed mom and dad with some money and that the family is going to rejoice in God's favor by spending some of it on a skiing trip. You travel to one of many cool family ski venues and buy lift tickets for $140.00. After a full day of skiing, you stop by a family oriented hot springs pool and relax your aching muscles costing $20.00. Then you splurge on the way home and enjoy a nice bison steak meal with your family and leave a generous tip in the spirit of joy. As opportunities arise during the day you teach the kids that this day is brought to them courtesy of a gracious and loving God who wants us to rejoice in celebration of his creation and blessings. What child would not be drawn to a God like this that makes joy a basic part of life? And, what marriage would not be strengthened by a commitment to rejoicing together in God's goodness?

The Poor Tithe

God gave Moses numerous commands to care for the poor with the goal of eradicating poverty from the nation. The poor tithe was instituted to be paid once every three years to the local Levite, the stranger, the fatherless and the widow. The payment of this Tithe was promised to bring God's blessing upon His people. (Deut 14:28-29) In other words the Israelites were not just to preach sin and repentance for the saving of the soul. Rather, they were to apply the word of God to every area of life including care of the poor.

Today those of us that live in the United States are living in the wealthiest country the world has ever known and the wealth disparity between the developed countries and the least developed countries is greater than it has ever been. And yet, it is easy for us to assume that the world is not that broken because we don't see the poverty every day. And to further complicate the problem, the evangelical church has had to overcome some serious errors from early in the twentieth century when we distanced ourselves from theological liberals who stood for the social gospel that was devoid of the message of redemption. As a result, we committed a tactical error and ended up in large scale retreat from the front lines of poverty alleviation. As the church retreated from this mission, we opened the door to government stepping in to fill the gap left by the church's absence and we got Lyndon Johnson's massive war on poverty devoid of relational and spiritual content.

It is tempting to throw up our hands and say the government is now taking care of the poor, but that is a cop out. Even a literal interpretation of the poor Tithe would seem to require only 3.3% of income to go to various poverty fighting causes because it was only given every three years. We have amazing opportunities for investing this money wisely today. My wife and I, for example, enjoy spending part of our poor Tithe on helping an orphanage in Kenya. Churches usually have diaconal funds that can use money locally. There are many choices and to rejoice in the opportunity to serve the poor is consistent with Jesus' reason for coming to earth to "preach good news to the poor… to proclaim freedom for the prisoners and recovery of sight for the blind, to release the oppressed, to proclaim the year of the Lord's favor. (Luke 4:17-21)

Practical Suggestion: You may not be aware of any worthy charities that meet the needs of the poor. A practice I have seen others do may be helpful to you. Philanthropy clubs can be formed that are similar to investment clubs that have been around for years teaching people how to invest their money in the stock market. In this case, however, the purpose is to learn about and invest in charities. A group of ten people might come together and have each participant contribute $500 or $1,000 to the group. The individual members would then take turns researching and presenting the case for investing in a particular charity. After each member has had a chance to make his or her case for a charity, the group will spend time deciding how many charities to support and how much to give until the fund is exhausted. It is an excellent way to learn about opportunities to wisely give your money in the fight against poverty and also to build new friendships with like-minded individuals. You could even do this within your family and have your teenagers do the research. As an alternative, I heartily recommend World magazine as a source for learning about a variety of Christian based organizations impacting the world for God's glory.

The Levitical Tithe

This tithe is what we commonly think of today when we say we are "giving our tithe" to support our local church. In the Old Testament it was given to the Levites for the services they performed for the congregation. (Leviticus 27:30-33, Numbers 18:20-24, 30-32, II Chronicles 31:4-6) This included services performed at the Tabernacle or in the Temple, but also for the education of the people and musicians among other uses of the money. The amount given for this purpose was 10% of the increase each year that we can translate in the New Testament context as what is to be given to the church.

Various surveys exist that measure the amount of giving that takes place in churches. One survey I am familiar with estimates that only 9% of adults who say they are born again contributed 10% or more of their income.[lxiii] This data begs the question of "why?" Why is it that Evangelicals, who hold to the literal truths of Scripture, are so closed fisted with their money when it comes to responding to the grace and mercy of the Gospel?

There are probably many answers to this question, but I am convinced that one reason for the pitiful giving of Evangelicals is the separation of giving from our relationship with God. If writing a check out to the church is seen on the same level as paying the trash bill, then it has no more significance in our lives than any other financial transaction. However, our giving to God should not seem like a transaction, it is relational. Giving should not be separated from worship of the triune God or it loses its significance as a spiritual discipline in our lives that can be used to draw us closer to God. If on my wife's birthday, for example, I am busy and decide to just give her a check like it is just one more bill to be paid rather than a gift that I had to put some thought into, the consequences might be significant. Why? Because her birthday is not just one more bill to be paid. We have a relationship and a gift to her needs to be intentional to be meaningful to her. How much more should our gift to God be intentional and meaningful?

In the Old Testament there is story after story of offerings being given as an act of worship in response to what God had done. Noah is one of the earliest examples of giving an offering to God soon after he is saved from the flood (Gen 8:20-21). God received that offering and gave a covenantal promise to us as a result. When the original temple was dedicated by Solomon, there were offerings given and received by God (II Chronicles 7:1). Offerings were a part of worship in contrition (I Chronicles 21:26) and covenant renewal (Joshua 8:31). In the New Testament, offerings to Jesus are personal and acts of worship (Luke 7:36-50). So the first principle of giving to the local church should be that it is done in the context of worship and a relationship.

But some might object that church leaders are not worthy of the money because of the way they use it. It seems that cynicism is rampant in not just the church, but in all parts of society, where almost every day has a new scandal revealed among government, military, church or sports leaders. It is easy to see why one could conclude that no one is worthy of our offerings. However, God does not ask us to give to Him based on the integrity of the pastor. Rather, our gift given in faith is to God. If the clergy misuse the offerings, we ought to use whatever rights we have to protest and call for reform, but that corruption in no way invalidates the act of faith in giving our offerings to God or justifies our failing to tithe.

Other reasons to practice the Levitical tithe are that it is appropriate to support pastors and other Christian workers with our resources (I Cor 9:4, Num 18:24). But besides the pragmatic necessity of supporting those who labor full time in church service, it is also important to note that the tithe belongs to the Lord. The Bible teaches it is stealing from God if we don't give it. "A tithe of everything from the land, whether grain from the soil or fruit from the trees, belongs to the Lord; it is holy to the Lord. Leviticus 27:30. Or consider Malachi 3: 8, "will a man rob God? Yet you rob me. But you ask, 'How do we rob you?' In tithes and offerings." Tithing is a regular reminder that God is our source of life and wealth.

To fail to acknowledge Him in giving the Levitical Tithe can be used as a diagnostic tool that points to something being deeply wrong with our relationship with God. In fact, it seems to me that the time of giving tithes and offerings in worship services is when the rubber meets the road. We can fake most elements of worship like singing or praying, but when the offering basket is passed we come face to face with the question of whether we believe all this gospel talk. To stop giving is a pretty good indication that we are just playing church and not really believing the whole gospel yet. Use your lack of a generous heart as a diagnostic tool for your soul.

On the other hand, there is another extreme that we need to guard against. It is also possible that we become above average in our charitable giving and we find our identity and righteousness in this instead of in Jesus. Our brokenness can lead us to take pride in our superior giving in comparison to others. This attitude is far from the gospel of redemption which should motivate us to give out of our love of Christ rather than to find some sort of self atoning sacrifice in our gifts.

Practical Suggestion: My wife and I find the most practical time to drop our offerings in the box is after communion. I believe that worship is a dialogue with God and in our church communion is next to last in the worship service. I have found that, after reflection on my own brokenness and the healing shalom offered by what Jesus did for me on the cross, I am most pliable to desire to give back something after communion. Your church may have a different order of worship, but I find it an incredibly important part of worship to be able to bring a gift to God as part of the exercise of worshiping Him each week. I Corinthians 16:2 seems to indicate that bringing a gift to God is an important part of any exercise of worship: "On the first day of every week, each one of you should set aside a sum of money in keeping with his income…"

The Balanced and Abundant Life

What happens if we just practice one of the tithes? We might become quite smug with giving in one area when we see others neglecting it. When we pick and choose or compare ourselves to others we end up unbalanced and in misery.

For example, what if we just focus on practicing the rejoicing tithe? We spend all our extra money on enjoying the good things God has given us to the exclusion of a concern for the poor or the needs of the church. We might be happy for awhile, but as we focus on gaining more and more pleasure and joy, we find that we receive it less and less. A pure pursuit of joy and happiness will not end well as it runs into the law of diminishing returns. Some call it a "hedonistic treadmill" that in the end wipes out our capacity for joy. We were not made to pursue selfish enjoyment to the exclusion of others and in the end we will be miserable because of our failure to serve others with our wealth.

But what if we pursue helping the poor only? Isn't that a way to the good life God intends for us? No, a life of rigid, gritting your teeth and helping the less fortunate is also not the life God intends for us. We are to have a major concern for the poor, but not at the exclusion of experiencing joy in our lives and our family's life. Furthermore, the foundation of growing the church is through discipleship of others that can only be done if pastors and teachers are funded to be able to fulfill their calling in teaching and preaching the gospel.

And what if we choose to only give our charitable dollars to the work of the church? Well, that is the course that many chose in the 20th century that led to the retreat from the war on poverty. When we see the gospel as only a fire insurance policy, we neglect the real world that is broken and in need of the healing message of the gospel to enjoy life and to meet the needs of the poor. Or, as we discussed in earlier chapters, if we neglect our businesses and give all our excess cash flow to the church, we impair God's plan to meet the needs of people through the production of "daily bread."

Surprising Rewards of Faithfulness in Giving

Because I am so opposed to the "health and prosperity gospel" which teaches God owes you success, I am hesitant to mention the blessings that flow from faithfulness to God's teaching on generosity. However, both Scripture and my personal observation confirm that God often does return our meager efforts in being generous with surprising blessings.

The scriptural support comes from many places, but in Malachi 3:10 we are encouraged to test God in His faithfulness if we will practice generosity, "Bring the whole tithe into the storehouse, that there may be food in my house. Test me in this," says the Lord Almighty, "and see if I will not throw open the floodgates of heaven and pour out so much blessing that you will not have room enough for it." Or II Corinthians 9:11, "You will be made rich in every way so that you can be generous on every occasion, and through us your generosity will result in thanksgiving to God."

While we can't expect to become rich just because we are Christians, I have found that Christians are blessed in surprising ways when they practice generosity when it may or may not make much sense from a practical point of view.

Many years ago my wife and I did not have much money, but our church had a special need. We decided that we should give $1,000 even though we could have used that money for a lot of other needs in our life. Two weeks after giving the money a letter arrived in the mail from a former employer that I hadn't heard from for about two years. Enclosed was a check for over $2,000 because the cover letter said I was wrongfully denied overtime for travel time when I worked for them. Wow! That was really moving when that money arrived, and I realized that our faithfulness had been rewarded with a check over two times what we had given to our church.

While that check blew my mind about God's faithfulness, I have found many Christian friends telling similar stories of God's faithfulness in times of need. I have a good friend, for example, who related a story of a trial his family went through when they moved to a new location to take a job which shortly thereafter was eliminated. This man had made some money and knew that he should tithe 10% on it even though he was facing unemployment. He went ahead and tithed his recent gain in faith even though he didn't know what his future employment would look like. At the same time he tried to refinance his house to gain some additional leverage and found to his surprise that his house had appreciated enough that he was able to get 10 times his tithe amount back in cash out refinancing. To this day he credits God with rewarding his faithfulness in tithing with that cash windfall when his family needed some additional funds.

I've heard many such stories about God's faithfulness being demonstrated in financial terms after tithing. One woman told me she was hesitant to tithe because she was in tough financial straits, but after stepping out in faith and giving money to her church, God provided her with a car that was above and beyond what she could have expected. Her comment to me was, "Why was I surprised that God would do this for me?"

10% of What?

In teaching biblical finance in churches a question inevitably comes up regarding what income should we tithe off of? Meaning, should we tithe off of our gross income before taxes or net income after taxes? I don't like this question because it tends to take the joy out of giving to focus on this detail and I find myself at odds with some other very good Christian teachers. However, I want to address it because I don't think Christian leaders should put an unnecessary burden on followers of Jesus. I think the answer is clear that God does not expect us to tithe off of money that we never have access to. In other words, we should only look at the net income we receive after taxes to determine what percentage of our income we want to give to rejoicing, poverty alleviation and churches.

I believe there are some very practical and biblical reasons for my position on this topic. God clearly says to tithe off of the increase of our labor. If we are a small business person and we sell goods and services of $1,000,000 no one expects us to tithe off of that gross amount. No, rather, we would deduct the cost of producing those goods and services first. The cost to buy the inventory that we sell may be $900,000 and the resulting income before taxes would be $100,000. If we tithed on the gross income, we would effectively wipe out any profit. No pastor or Christian teacher would suggest that we tithe off of the gross revenue amount.

When it comes to taxes however, some Christian teachers believe that they should be excluded from the formula. I think they are missing the point of God's teaching on tithing. Taxes are also just a cost of doing business. They are paid to provide national defense, a judicial system that promotes the rule of law and other services we expect out of our government that allow businesses to operate. Additionally, this teaching is naïve in forgetting that at times the margin tax rates has been 90% or higher thereby creating a situation where a Christian business person could be underwater in cash flow for each incremental dollar of sales she creates if tithing is done off of pretax profits.[lxiv] Tithing is just a baseline and there is no prohibition in giving generously off of more than

10% of our increase that is sometimes differentiated as offerings. However, teachers of the Bible should be careful to not go beyond the requirements that God lays down.

How to Get Started

I have counseled with new Christians who have never heard of the idea of tithing and are shocked by the idea that God might require 10% or more of their income as an act of worship. I am sympathetic to their reaction. It is good to crawl before we walk and it's important to remember that our giving does not increase God's love for us by even one iota. Therefore I always encourage new Christians, or old Christians that have never practiced tithing, to just begin with something. Giving as an act of worship is the place to start in discipleship. Once that practice is established, the amount to be given can be slowly ingrained in a sincere Christian's heart as they look to the Scriptures and become convinced of God's way for living life and plan for the money that flows into it. So if this chapter is foreign to you, I would encourage you to get started by giving something as an act of worship to the God you love. It doesn't matter how much, but rather that you are giving in response to the ultimate act of love that God gave to you. Details of the debits and credits of how much you should give will follow naturally as you grow in the knowledge of the grace of God's love for you.

Summary

Giving money is a touchy topic for churches to speak on because of the invasiveness of the topic into our private lives. However, the Bible speaks clearly to us on this area. We should evaluate our hearts and lives in regard to the level of concern we show by how we spend our money on celebratory activities, poverty alleviation and support for the work of the church in teaching and preaching.

Discussion questions

1. Describe the level of joy in your life. What does this indicate about the realty of Jesus' presence in your daily living?
2. How could you better utilize your money to rejoice?
3. Why is concern for the poor important to God? What is he calling you to do in this area?
4. Why do you think so few people actually give 10%? What can be done to improve this percentage?
5. Is your charitable giving transactional or relational? Why?
6. How can you better reflect joy, concern for the poor and God's church in your giving?

PART IV

Your Legacy

CHAPTER 10

Inheritance: Passing It On

I hated all my toil in which I toil under the sun, seeing that I must leave it to the man who will come after me, [19] and who knows whether he will be wise or a fool? Yet he will be master of all for which I toiled and used my wisdom under the sun. This also is vanity.

Ecclesiastes 2:18-19

A good person leaves an inheritance for their children's children, but a sinner's wealth is stored up for the righteous.

Proverbs 13:22

Inheritance matters are incredibly controversial. Whether it's politicians polarizing comments on the need to have higher estate taxes, or bumper stickers on RV's that create both smiles and smirks by proclaiming, "I'm spending my children's inheritance," there is a lot of noise to sort through on this topic. Moreover, there is the emotional distress created for some parents in even thinking about discussing their money with their children, and vice versa. Or, with the increase in blended families today, some estate lawyers will not even assist families trying to work through inheritance matters because of the highly emotional nature of trying to be fair to everyone. Therefore it's important to look at what discerning wisdom the Bible provides on this topic as we think about what happens to our wealth when we pass onto a better place.

One truth is certain; a poorly thought out inheritance plan can create disastrous results for the recipients. Take Lynn for example. She attended my church and was constantly in financial distress caused primarily by a lack of financial discipline that kept her living above her means and in constant turmoil. Then one day her mother died and she inherited over $100,000. She thought she was the one who had died and gone to heaven because the inheritance seemed like enough money to live on forever. "Forever" took about six months as she successfully went through every penny of her mother's lifetime of savings before returning to her life of poverty. After the spending spree, only an accumulation of depreciating "stuff" showed evidence that her life was touched by a windfall.

On the other hand, I have seen many successful transitions of productive assets being passed down to children who build on the lifetime of capital their parents had produced. Many farms and other small businesses, for example, have been kept in the same family for generations because of virtuous family values like hard work and thrift being passed down along with title to the family business and bank account. Or, many Christian and other charitable organizations receive great benefit from the willingness of donors to include them in their wills. A wise estate plan can be your last act in this life to pass on peace through your finances to those around you.

Unfortunately, there isn't a one-size-fits-all plan for inheritance issues because of the complexity of each situation. Every family will be different. Some children will be trustworthy and some not. The size of the family's wealth will impact decision making. A desire to leave money to charities will need to be considered, and tax laws will always change requiring periodic reviews of the actual plan to ensure it still meets the goals it is designed for. These are just a few of the variables that require wisdom and prayer to best achieve kingdom objectives when you pass on your wealth. Furthermore, we need to humbly remember that we can't control what happens to our money from the grave as the author of Ecclesiastes laments. However, we should gain an understanding of God's view of inheritance matters and attempt, as good stewards of whatever wealth we have been entrusted, to pass it on in the manner that would bring Him the most glory.

Principle 1: God believes in giving an inheritance

Even a cursory review of the Bible would show that the concept of "inheritance" is an important theme. I think it's proper to say the Bible celebrates inheritance. The word itself appears over 200 times in the Bible, and including the concept of heirs would increase that number significantly. In the Old Testament there were many laws of inheritance linked to blood line, but the focus was on God's promise to Abraham where the land of Canaan was given to him and his descendants forever. As the Bible unfolds, the promised inheritance to the faithful is enlarged to include the entire world (Ps 2:8, Romans 4:13). In the New Testament that concept was greatly enriched to include the acquisition of spiritual blessings and promises from God. For example, eternal life and the kingdom of God are phrases used to describe our joyful and eternal inheritance in a place that "can never perish, spoil or fade." (I Peter 1:4)

My point here is not to go into a full exposition of how the term "inheritance" is used in the Bible. Rather, it is to point out that any discussion of the more mundane matter of how we should pass on our wealth should be rooted in an understanding that God sees giving an inheritance as a good thing. His example of providing an inheritance for us, his children, is one way he demonstrates his love as our Father. As we seek to imitate God in our lives, his example of providing for his children through an inheritance should give us encouragement that it is a worthy and good thing to do. We should reject the advice of those who might encourage us to spend our children's inheritance on ourselves as contrary to the spirit of Christ.

Principle 2: An inheritance is not just about the money

Nancy and I went to a fund raising dinner about 30 years ago for a Christian school that deeply impacted our thinking about parenting and inheritance. The speaker used as his text Proverbs 13:22, "A good person leaves an inheritance for his children's children…" I had heard that verse before, but I had never really considered that it didn't make a lot of sense in the context of the Old Testament laws regarding inheritance. There are no laws about leaving the land or anything else to your grandchildren, so what does this verse mean? The speaker went on to lay out a compelling case that the verse is really about leaving a non-monetary heritage to your children that will carry onto their children and to many generations following. Wow! That thought really clicked with us as we began to think about all the things we hoped could be passed on to our grandchildren such as our faith. But it was much more than just a simple faith in Jesus; it was a comprehensive worldview that reflects God's revelation of subduing the earth through productive work, wisdom, love, grace, adventures, stories and friendships. Now that our children are almost all raised, we are so grateful when we see fruits of God's grace in their lives. We know that whatever money we are able to pass along to them, it pales in comparison to the chance we've had to impart the Christian faith and worldview into their thinking. I would encourage anyone reading this to focus first on the multi-generational aspects of the inheritance you will pass on to your descendants.

Principle 3: Monetary inheritance should be granted thoughtfully and gradually

The Bible warns of the dangers of giving an inheritance all at once: "An inheritance quickly gained at the beginning, will not be blessed in the end." (Pr 20:21) Nancy and I have also considered a complementary Scriptural principle for giving money to children from the parable of the talents, "You have been faithful with a few things; I will put you in charge of many." Like my friend Lynn who I described earlier, those who are not faithful stewards with modest income do not suddenly become Warren Buffett when they are given a large inheritance. However, as parents, we can give modest incentives to our children to watch them grow in competence preparing them for more and more responsibility with financial matters.

There are many techniques to gradually coach your children with money. Some of our successes have come by offering to match money our kids raised for the purchase of their first car. This process turned them into entrepreneurs as we have enjoyed watching businesses spring up in babysitting, car cleaning, lawn mowing and pet sitting to name a few. The matching offer also seemed to stimulate the motivation to find part time work in various places such as fast food, movie theaters and other retail businesses. And when E-bay and Amazon came into existence we saw our first internet business spring up.

College is another excellent opportunity to pass on and observe the results of an early inheritance. Student loan debt recently surpassed the *$1,000,000,000,000* mark and is strangling many graduates trying to start a life after college.[lxv] We didn't want to see our kids start off their working life with a large student debt burden so it provided an opportunity for Nancy and me to bless our children with tuition assistance. However, as with other assistance, goofing off on mom and dad's dime won't last more than a semester. As our children demonstrate their faithfulness, they are given more and more of their inheritance early in the form of money for room, board and tuition. So in practice, if they have a good semester, they are likely going to have the next one paid for them. But if it's obvious that our son or daughter was not a serious student, then it's just as important that they learn the other part of the parable of the talents in that the unfaithful servant was cut off. "You wicked lazy servant!...Take the talent from him..." As our children learn that our unconditional love doesn't equate to an open checkbook when not living a productive life, they aren't tempted as much to lead the life of a sluggard.

As some of our children have now formed their own families, Nancy and I have the chance to continue our gradual transfer of wealth to them. For example, many people take out small whole life insurance policies on their children when they are born. We happened to do that and now they have grown to be worth several thousand dollars in cash value. We plan on giving those policies to our children now that they are married. Or, when they buy their first house, we might consider assisting with the down payment. 529 plans are a wonderful tax advantaged invention that also allows anyone to help plan for future college expenses, so I expect if we have grandchildren that we will be looking at that as an early inheritance project.

Everyone's plan will be different depending on the resources you have and your children's maturity, but slow and responsible transfers seem biblical and practical. One caution, however: I have seen parents attempt to micromanage their married children through money. Boundaries are important in allowing married couples to flourish without using money to obtain parental control.

In summary, I think it's interesting to note that when God talks about the godly man in the Psalms, he doesn't necessarily emphasize how important that man will be, but it is the children of the godly that grow in stature, "His children will be mighty in the land." (Ps 112:2) That should be the hope of the Christian couple as they begin to pass on their inheritance and let their children build on their capital that they might become mighty in the land.

Principle 4: It's okay to leave different amounts to different children at different times

There seems to be an unwritten rule somewhere that parents are obligated to give every child exactly the same inheritance. I'm not sure where that rule is written, but it's not the Bible. Inheritance is a privilege, not a right. The size of the grant is up to the parents and not the beneficiary. In fact, as my oldest brother used to enjoy pointing out, Deuteronomy 21 actually taught that the oldest son should get a double inheritance. While those judicial laws were for a particular place and time, they still contain wisdom that we can learn from. For example, the Bible commentaries I have read on that passage believe it points to the wisdom of rewarding the oldest because he was given the primary responsibility for caring for the needs of the parents. In the 21st century I could see the parents of several children deciding to give more to the child that was most involved in caring for their needs in their old age. Or, if one child is a successful orthopedic surgeon making a million dollars a year and another child is a missionary to Kenya barely making it, it seems that a family counsel could be convened to discuss a variation in disbursing the family assets from the norm.

But a more poignant question is whether a child should ever be disinherited. This is a very tough issue and one that requires much prayer, wisdom and counsel. However, I believe this option must be considered if you approach these decisions from the stewardship perspective. Your wealth is not really your wealth, but God's money that has been entrusted to you. If you are truly only managing what you have been given from God, then this question has a much different perspective than a non-Christian would have. If we think of the money as ours, we probably love all of them the same and do not want to be perceived as showing favoritism. However, if the money is God's, does it make good sense to give it to a child that might have left the Christian faith and is living a life in direct defiance of God's revealed will?

This is a very difficult question and there are a lot of possible ways to look at it even if you are committed to the stewardship view of wealth. For example, many young people leave the faith only to come back at a later date after sowing wild oats and reaping the inevitable harvest. Lawyers are able to design wills to hold off on payments of money for extended periods of time. For example, if a young adult becomes addicted to alcohol or drugs and continues to live in defiance of God's commandments up to age 45, a will might dictate that they could lose their inheritance. However, if they overcome the addiction and exhibit signs of Christian grace in their lives they could have some arbitrator decide to pay the inheritance over a period of time.

I won't pretend to give legal advice, but this question is one that should be wrestled with in your consideration of where God's money should go once you are no longer a steward over it. A wise lawyer can help you wordsmith your intentions in this area.

Principle 5: Get a will and other final legal documents in place

I have seen some estimates that show only about half of Americans have a will.[lxvi] It would be wonderful if we could know when we are going to die and have all of our money disbursed on that day. However, we don't know the day or hour that God will call us home so it's important to have our legal documents in order. Otherwise the state will be the one making the decisions on who will raise our children and how our money will be divided. As stewards, it's our duty to make these decisions and ensure that we further God's kingdom with our decisions. Find a good lawyer and make a will to deal with your end of life financial matters. A lawyer will also advise you on other important documents such as a durable power of attorney, a living will and a power of attorney for health care or any other necessary documents for your specific state.

We've only talked about leaving money to our children up to this point, but a will is also a useful tool to designate money to charitable works. Warren Buffett once said that he wanted "to give my kids enough so that they could feel that they could do anything, but not so much that they could do nothing." I think that's a thoughtful saying to give us some perspective on how much inheritance is enough for our kids. We are under no obligation to give any particular percentage of our wealth to our kids, but as the thrust of this chapter notes, some inheritance is biblical to give. However, it is also biblical to be generous to other Christian works that are also bringing in the kingdom of God. Once again, wisdom, prayer and counsel are important before going to the lawyer with your distribution plan.

If you cannot afford a lawyer to draw up a will I suggest that you consult some of the legal form companies that offer online services. I have had estate lawyers comment that they send people to these sites if they cannot afford their services because they feel they are generally very good.

Principle 6: Life Insurance- Get it!

A former customer of mine died in a tragic car accident leaving a wife and children behind. Not only was it a terrible emotional blow to his wife to lose her spouse, but he also had a business with significant debt. She didn't know how to run the business and so she was left with the additional burden of managing the business and the debt payments. The accident couldn't have been avoided, but leaving this poor widow behind with debt was inexcusable with the inexpensive price of term life insurance today.

This responsibility is a biblical one. I Timothy 5:8 says "if anyone does not provide for his relatives, especially for his immediate family, he has denied the faith and is worse than an unbeliever." That's a strong statement, but it underscores the importance of taking advantage of the risk management tools available today like life and disability insurance to safeguard our families from financial disaster. Life insurance is not a lack of faith. Rather it is a prudent tool to fulfill our duty to our family and to keep from putting our church or government in a position of having to care for our spouse and children.

So how much life insurance is needed? Some use a rule of thumb of suggesting 10 times your annual income. That's not a great way to estimate your life insurance needs because everyone is unique and your number might be much higher or lower. It's best to consult with a trusted insurance specialist who can help you work through your need of life insurance. Also, Crown Financial Ministries has a helpful life insurance need calculator that you can use to get a good estimate at: http://www.crown.org/Resources/Personal/Calculators/LlifeInsuranceNeed.aspx. This calculator will ask you to estimate various costs you might leave your spouse with such as: funeral expenses, debts, college and annual living expenses. It will also help you think through benefits such as social security that will begin paying out upon your death.

You might be surprised at how much life insurance you could need. It could be as high as $1,000,000 or more if you are young with children to support. That might sound like an insurmountable amount that you could never afford. However, I ran some numbers off an internet advertisement for a 30 year old male that doesn't smoke and is in good health and I got back some estimates for $1,400,000 of 20 year term insurance for a premium of only $50.00 a month. Now that's off the internet and your numbers may be different, but the point is that it's incredibly cheap. As an act of love for your family you should work through your own numbers and try to cover your family's exposure to the loss of income that would occur if you died.

Principle 7: Honoring an Inheritance Received

Have you ever received an inheritance? I have received two small inheritances and I found them both to be emotional experiences. The first inheritance I received was from the Aunt Roellen and Uncle Virl who were the farmers who lost all their money in the Great Depression that I discussed in Chapter 4. While the amount of the check was only a few thousand, the thoughts that ran through my mind were about all the hard work that went into their lives and that this represented a gift to me of their life energy. I felt an overwhelming desire to use that money wisely because I knew how hard they had worked for it. My mother and father also left me a small inheritance that similarly moved me to appreciate their life.

We had an opportunity to teach our kids about inheritance when my older brother died in 2006. He was a single man, and he left each of my five children around $10,000. We were able to impress on each of them the importance of honoring Uncle John with how they spend his gift to them. This was a very teachable moment and I am proud of how my kids responded to our counsel. One of them used the money to earn a master's degree. Another put the money to work as part of the down payment on his first house. Two kids were able to use part of it to help purchase a car so they could have transportation to their work and school, and one of our boys has kept it invested waiting for the right opportunity to use it in a way that Uncle John would approve of.

While you may never have an opportunity to actually experience being on the receiving end of a monetary inheritance, we all have a way to practice the gracious acceptance of a spiritual inheritance as we reflect on the work of Jesus on the cross for us. If we are fortunate enough to enjoy a worldly inheritance we should also use it as a reminder of the greater spiritual inheritance that we will one day enjoy.

Summary

I hope that this book has inspired you in some way to make a lot of money and to be able to enjoy it through saving, spending or giving it away. However, as I get older I've noticed that I am growing more interested in thinking about what kind of legacy I will leave on this earth. There is much more to our legacy than just money, but it is also a part of what we will leave behind. God's word puts a lot of emphasis on the inheritance He has given us and I think that example implores us to give thought to our legacy. As in all things this book has considered, we should approach this question from a stewardship perspective. Hopefully this chapter has stimulated some of your thinking to align your wealth disbursement plans with your eternal hope of an "inheritance which is imperishable and will not fade away, reserved in heaven for you." I Peter 1:4

Discussion Questions

1. Why does the Bible speak so often about inheritance matters? What does our inheritance we will receive from God teach us about his nature?
2. How can an inheritance ruin someone? What are some techniques we might try to use to avoid the potential negative results of an inheritance?
3. What are the non-monetary things you hope to leave your children as their inheritance? How are you going about giving them that inheritance today?
4. In what ways are you giving your children an early inheritance? Are they responding in a way that encourages you to entrust them with more of your assets when you die?
5. Have you talked to your children about your philosophy of inheritance? Why or why not?
6. Is it okay to leave different amounts of money to different children? Why or why not?
7. Do you have a will? If not, what action steps can you take this week to put one in place?
8. Calculate how much life insurance you need. If you do not have enough coverage, what steps can you take to protect your family in this important area?
9. Do you believe God has an eternal inheritance prepared for you? What hope or despair does your answer leave you with?

CONCLUSION

Where Do We Go From Here?

> *Now all has been heard: here is the conclusion of the matter: Fear God and keep his commandments, for this is the duty of all mankind.*
>
> Ecclesiastes 12:13

My prayer is that something in this book has been helpful to you. Nancy and I have learned these principles over 35 years of married life raising five children along the way. In the early days we were basically broke, with no net worth, and in these later days we have much more than we ever could have imagined when we first got married. I can honestly say that in times of plenty and in times of want, we've lived with peace regarding finances in our marriage. Not that I haven't done a lot of stupid things with money that probably annoyed my gracious wife, but we've always been united in what we were trying to accomplish in life, and money has been subordinate to those life purposes. I hope that this book has given you the tools to similarly develop your financial plans around the higher calling you have been given in your time on this earth. That alone will put money in it's proper place in your life—a tool to be used by you in living a celebratory, purposeful life, rather than a demanding and unforgiving idol.

I can also attest to the comfort these biblical principles can provide in times of unexpected stress. About 11 years ago I remember going to my mailbox and pulling out a letter from a big St. Louis law firm. The letter inside said I was being sued for an amount far in excess of our net worth for something that I had no responsibility for. I did not have a clue I was a target of a lawsuit until I opened that letter. After engaging legal counsel I was not able to get the lawsuit thrown out. It went on for several years and included a very unpleasant experience of being deposed by fifteen lawyers sitting around a table. The stress of living with the possibility of financial ruin was something I will admit that I lost some sleep over. However, in God's Providence, he used that experience to remind me of the foundational doctrine taught in this book: its God's wealth and not mine. As I relearned that valuable concept of stewardship, the stress of the lawsuit lessened and I was once again comforted in the belief that God was in control of the lawsuit and His wealth. Whatever happened, I would focus on what I could control: my duty to fear God and keep his commandments as the writer of Ecclesiastes encourages. Years later the lawsuit was finally dismissed against me, but the whole process brought a time of personal spiritual growth. I learned again the folly of trusting in my wealth instead of the true source of my security. Money was a useful diagnostic tool of my spiritual health in a very poignant way for me as I came face to face with the prospect of losing everything. I hope you never have such an experience, but when unexpected storms of life hit, my prayer is that this book may have been helpful in giving you a solid foundation that can withstand them.

As a final note, I want to leave you with a thought we discussed early in the book. As I've covered this material in small groups,

Where Do We Go From Here?

I sometimes find that it can be discouraging to those who have made a lot of mistakes up to this point in their financial lives. It's easy to get down on ourselves for not having been more diligent, smarter and productive. But, of course, we've all made many mistakes financially and otherwise in life. In fact, the point of the Christian gospel is not that we somehow earn our righteousness by working harder and harder at being good to make up for past wrongs, but rather that we cast ourselves on the mercy of Jesus whose righteousness is perfect and it covers our past, present and future sins. We can then move forward, having gained our new identity in one who was perfect and who covers our sins with his mercy and grace. So my final word is to forget what lies behind and begin moving forward in the power of your transformed life.

Best wishes to you in the start of your new financial adventure. Now Onward!

APPENDIX A

Smart Money with Purpose Report Card

Successful money management that integrates the spiritual with the practical aspects of our finances will include virtually all dimensions of a person's life: purpose, attitude toward wealth, acceptance of a "stewardship" mindset, psychological wiring, income and spending philosophy, debt management, investing habits, generosity, marital harmony and legacy planning. And this list is by no means exhaustive.

Now that you've completed the book and have had a chance to reflect on many of these topics as they relate to you, it's time to assess your progress. Listed below are 20 questions--two from each chapter's material. You should go through each question and assign a score from 1 to 5 for each. A "1" would mean you give yourself an "F" on that topic and you recognize that it needs a lot of work. A "5" means you give yourself an "A" because you believe you are living with peace regarding finances as that topic relates to your standing before God and your personal calling in life.

As you complete this exercise, it will be most beneficial if you have a close friend who has some financial training that you could review the results with. The purpose of the report card is to help raise awareness about your current relationship with money. A trusted friend would be helpful for you in processing the results of this exercise as you prayerfully seek to transform areas where you still struggle. Coaching questions might include: What areas would you most like to improve? What would it take to make it happen? What is the biggest impediment to successfully changing? What action steps can you take? Is there someone you can be accountable to?

If you score a perfect 100, you can probably skip this step, but for the rest of us, this will hopefully guide us to areas we can still take practical or spiritual steps to better fully integrate our faith with our financial management.

1. How strong is your belief that money is intrinsically good? Can you articulate Biblical reasons why? Does this belief impact the way you live? _____
2. How well does your life reflect Jesus' celebratory attitude that included joyful "eating and drinking" in his time on earth? Does the way you spend money reflect this joyful attitude toward life? _____
3. Have you grown beyond the temptation to believe that with "just a little more" money my problems could be solved and I would be happier? Or does the allure of money still have a deceptive hold on your life? _____
4. How much do you see yourself as a steward or trustee over what God has given you to manage? Or do you still think of money as "yours" to do whatever you want with it?
   _____
5. Do you have one or more clear "callings" or "purposes" in your life that are the driving factors in how you manage your money? Do you have a clear purpose statement(s)? Or are

your money practices unconnected to a feeling of what God has placed you on this earth to accomplish? _____
6. Have you accepted the Reformation view that all people are uniquely gifted by God to serve others in a calling that we are to pursue? Or, have you adopted the 21st Century mindset to pursue our own interests whether they help others or not? _____
7. Have you written your inner story about your relationship with money and examined it critically to determine if you are still holding to deep money beliefs that are childish? Is your inner story that guides your money decisions leading you to make wise money decisions? _____
8. Have you considered your money type (from Ch 4 quiz) and recognized weaknesses that need to be mitigated? If married, have you come to understand your spouse better now that you know the strengths and weaknesses of your money type and his/hers? _____
9. Have you done the five money consciousness exercises in Chapter 5 for yourself? Has it changed your spending behavior as you reorient your thinking to consider money as what you spend your "life energy" on? Is it causing you to live a more intentional life? _____
10. Are you aware of what resources you would need to attain financial independence? Is this a legitimate goal for you to pursue? Can you articulate why or why not clearly? _____
11. The three biggest expenses for a household can be children, house and car decisions. Are you confident that the next time one of these is an issue that you have a solid plan to be a good steward in your decision making? _____

12. Three ways to budget were discussed in chapter 6. Do you have a budget process in place and is it working to help you reach your objectives? _____
13. If you have debt, do you have a plan to pay off as quickly as possible the two types of debt defined as "regrettable" and "immoral" in chapter 7? Are you making progress? (If you have no regrettable or immoral debt, you can give yourself a "5".) _____
14. Do you have a system of debt management in place to monitor your credit score and take reasonable steps to keep it high, evaluate new debt in light of your budget and not rule of thumb suggestions, and refinance debt when rates are low? _____
15. Have you identified the time frames within which you will need funds from investments and put them in buckets for asset allocation purposes as discussed in chapter 8? And have you identified any concentrations of investments that may be placing you at unnecessary risk that could be mitigated by diversifying your investments? Do you know the costs you are being charged for your investments so you can ensure you are getting the best value? _____
16. Have you exhausted productive investments you could make in your own calling before making investments in other places? _____
17. What is your level of joy in your giving? _____
18. Are you addressing in some way in your budget donations the 3 principle areas encouraged in the Bible: to joyfully celebrate God's goodness, taking care of the poor and supporting of worship and teaching? Do you meet the 10% biblical minimum of giving of your increase each year? _____

19. Do you have a will, durable power of attorney and a health care power of attorney in place? _____
20. Have you estimated how much life and disability insurance you should have and purchased it? _____

Notes

My Journey

i Ronald J. Sider, *Rich Christians in an Age of Hunger: A Biblical Study* (Downers Grove, IL: Inter-Varsity Press, 1977)

ii David Chilton, *Productive Christians in an Age of Guilt-Manipulators: A Biblical Response to Ronald J. Sider* (Tyler, Tx: Institute for Christian Economics, 1981)

Chapter 1

iii Gallop Daily: US Consumer Spending, July 25, 2013

iv The Economist, March 3, 2012, "A Fall to Cheer."

v Ibid. iv.

vi The Economist, June 1, 2013, "Towards the End of Poverty."

vii Adam Smith, *Theory of Moral Sentiments*, 1759

viii Credit Union Times, August 8, 2013, "Do CU CEO's Really Earn More Than Bankers?" Heather Anderson

ix American Institute of Philanthropy, 2013, Top 25 Compensation Packages

x The Gospel Coalition, March 12, 2013, C.S. Lewis on Selfishness vs. Self Interest

xi Max Weber, *The Protestant Ethic and the Spirit of Capitalism,* Unwin Hyman, London and Boston, 1930

xii International Sociological Association, 1998

xiii John Wesley, The Use of Money, 1744

[xiv] The American Vision, May 7, 2014, "Do You Polish the Brass on a Sinking Ship?" Joel McDurmon

[xv] Steve Corbett and Brian Fikkert, *When Helping Hurts*, Moody Publishers, 2012

[xvi] One News Page, August 13, 2013, "U2's Bono hails Capitalism to Help the Hungry"

[xvii] John Mackey and Raj Sisodia, *Conscious Capitalism*, Harvard business Review Press, 2014

[xviii] Ibid., xvii

[xix] Ibid, xvii

[xx] The Christian Post, May 18, 2011, Scholar, China Notices Link Between Christianity, U.S. Economic Success

[xxi] Brian Griffiths, *The Creation of Wealth*, (Downers Grove, IL : Inter-Varsity press, 1984)

Chapter 2

[xxii] Barron's, June 2, 2014, "A Wealth of Misconceptions," Donald J. Boudreaux

[xxiii] The New Yorker, March 22, 2010, "Everybody Have Fun," Elizabeth Kolbert

[xxiv] Joe Dominguez and Vicki Robin, *Your Money or Your Life*, PP 8 (New York, NY, Penguin Group 1992)

[xxv] P. Brickman and D.T. Campbell, 1971, Hedonic relativism and planning the good society

[xxvi] Time, September 6, 2010, Do We Need $75,000 a year to Be Happy?

[xxvii] Westminster Shorter Catechism, 1647

[xxviii] Global Insight, November 2, 2005, The Economic Impact of Wal-Mart

Chapter 3

xxix Modern Reformation, Nov./Dec. 2007 Vol. 16, Our Calling and God's Glory, Gene Edward Veith

xxx Cotton Mather, A Christian and His Calling, 1701

xxxi Max Lucado, *Cure for the Common Life*, (Nashville, Tn, Thomas Nelson, 2005)

Chapter 4

xxxii Charles Dickens, *A Christmas Carol*, (Chapman and Hall, 1843)

xxxiii Brent Kessel, *It's not about the Money*, (New York, NY, HarperCollins, 2008)

Chapter 5

xxxiv Journal of Financial Planning, William P. Bengen, October 1994, "Calculating "safe" withdrawal rates and asset allocations based on historical data."

xxxv Joe Dominguez and Vicki Robin, *Your Money or Your Life*, (New York, NY, Penguin Group 1992)

xxxvi Jeff Yeager, *The Ultimate Cheapskate's Road Map to True Riches*, (New York, NY, Broadway Books, 2008)

Chapter 6

xxxvii Ehrlich, Paul R. (1968). *The Population Bomb*. Ballantine Books

xxxviii The Wall Street Journal, February 12, 2013, "America's Baby Bust," Jonathan V. Last

xxxix Ibid., xxxviii

xl USA Today, February 13, 2013, "As US Birth Rate Drops, Concern for the Future Mounts"

xli Kiplinger Magazine, June 2014, "Save for a House"

[xlii] Ibid, xli
[xliii] Bankrate.com., The Basics of Private Mortgage Insurance, April 25, 2013
[xliv] National Resources Defense Council, February 9, 2013, "What's going on with new home sizes – is the madness finally over?" Kaid Benfield's blog
[xlv] George S. Clason, *The Richest Man in Babylon,* (Penguin Books 1955)

Chapter 7
[xlvi] Aristotle, Politics, Book 1 Part X, 350 B.C.
[xlvii] Wayne A.M. Visser and Alastair McIntosh, July 1998, pp. 175-189, "A Short Review of the Historical Critique of Usury."
[xlviii] Ibid, xlvii
[xlix] Pope Benedict xiv, November 1, 1745, Vix Pervenit: On usury and other dishonest profit
[l] Mises Daily, February 18, 2010, The Economics of Calvin and Calvinism, Murray N. Rothbard
[li] Board of Governors of the Federal Reserve System, Charge-off and Delinquency Rates on Loans and Leases at Commercial Banks
[lii] The Institute for College & Success, December 2013, "Student Debt and the Class of 2012

Chapter 8
[liii] Berkshire Hathaway annual report, February 28, 2014
[liv] American Association of Individual Investors, May 2014, Peculiar Facts From 500 Years of Finance
[lv] Ted Williams, *The Science of Hitting,* (Touchstone 1986)
[lvi] 12 Value stocks.com, January 3, 2012, Things that Warren Buffett Learned from Ted Williams

[lvii] The Wall Street Journal, July 3, 2014, "Fee Gap Found for Pensions" Michael Corkery

[lviii] Fortune, February 5, 2014, "Buffett widens lead in $1 million hedge fund bet," Carol Loomis

[lix] The Wall Street Journal, February 15, 2014, "Whose Training Your Retirement navigator?" Jason Zweig

[lx] Ibid., liii

[lxi] Ibid., liii

Chapter 9

[lxii] Edward A. Powell and Rousas John Rushdoony, *Tithing and Dominion* (Vallecito, California: Ross House Books, 1979)

[lxiii] Barna Group, April 14, 2008, new Study Shows Trends in Tithing and Donating

[lxiv] Tax Foundation, October 1, 2008, Top Federal Tax Rate Was Once Over 90 Percent, Joseph Henchman

Chapter 10

[lxv] The Chronicle of Higher Education, July 17, 2013, "Federal Student-Loan Debt Crosses $1-Trillion Threshold," Cory Weinberg

[lxvi] USA Today, April 30, 2012, Times Change Wills, Yet Many Americans don't Have One, Christine Dugas

Made in the USA
Middletown, DE
28 September 2015